Answering the 8 Cries
of the Spirited
Child

DAVID *and* CLAUDIA ARP

Answering the 8 Cries
of the Spirited
Child

Strong Children Need
Confident Parents

HOWARD
PUBLISHING CO.

Our purpose at Howard Publishing is to:

- *Increase faith* in the hearts of growing Christians
- *Inspire holiness* in the lives of believers
- *Instill hope* in the hearts of struggling people everywhere

Because He's coming again!

Answering the 8 Cries of the Spirited Child © 2003 by David and Claudia Arp
All rights reserved. Printed in the United States of America
Published by Howard Publishing Co., Inc.
3117 North 7th Street, West Monroe, Louisiana 71291-2227
In association with the literary agency of Alive Communications, Inc., 7680 Goddard Street, Suite 200, Colorado Springs, CO 80920

03 04 05 06 07 08 09 10 11 12   10 9 8 7 6 5 4 3 2 1

Edited by Michele Buckingham
Interior design by John Luke
Cover design by Smart Guys Design

The names and identifying details of the individuals in the stories within have been changed to protect their privacy.

Library of Congress Cataloging-in-Publication Data
Arp, Dave
   Answering the 8 Cries of the spirited child : strong children need confident parents / David and Claudia Arp.
      p. cm.
   ISBN: 1-58229-284-1
   1. Problem children. 2. Child rearing. 3. Parenting. 4. Parent and child. I. Title: Answering the eight cries of the spirited child. II. Arp, Claudia. III. Title.

HQ773 .A74 2002
649'.153—dc21

2002192245

DEDICATION

To all parents who are blessed with a
spirited child. May this book give you
the confidence to love, lead, and
enjoy your strong child.

Table of Contents

ACKNOWLEDGMENTS

We are deeply indebted to the many people who contributed to this project and gratefully acknowledge the contributions of the following people:

To those in PEP Groups for Parents over the years as well as the parents who participated in our Spirited Child Survey, especially the moms at Cedar Springs Presbyterian Church, Knoxville, Tennessee. Thank you for sharing your questions, concerns, struggles, stories, and helpful tips for guiding and loving your own spirited children.

To those who have pioneered parent education and on whose shoulders we stand; including James Dobson, Kevin Leman, Randy Carlson, Gary Smalley, Emily Scott-Lowe, Dennis Lowe, John Trent, Ross Campbell, Henry Cloud, Nick Stinnett, John Defrain, John Townsend, John Gottman, Lawrence Kutner, T. Berry Brazelton, Mary Sheedy Kurcinka, and the many other researchers and authors from whom we quoted; for your sound work that gives a solid base for the cause for parent education.

To our Howard publishing team who has believed and supported this project with great enthusiasm. We especially thank our publisher, John Howard; our editors, Philis Boultinghouse and Michele

Buckingham, for their excellent editorial work; and Gary Myers and Debbie Webb for their great efforts to get the word out about this book.

To Brunnen Verlag, for having the vision for this book and publishing it first in German. We especially thank our publisher, Wilfried Jerke; editor, Renate Huebsch; and general manager, Detlef Holtgrefe, for your insights and encouragement.

To our friends who gave so much to this project, including Rich and Pam Batten, Emily Scott-Lowe, Friederike Klenk, Ursula Heim, Francine Smalley, Gabbi Horst, Clark and Ann Peddicord, Elke Pechmann, Annette Richter, and Barbara Mogel.

To our literary agent, Greg Johnson, of Alive Communications, for being our advocate and encouraging us along the way.

Help, I'm the Parent *of a* Spirited Child!

Over a cup of coffee, our friend Lisa related the following story:

> I was outside doing yard work when the fight broke out. I
> turned to see Patrick, my eight-year-old son, push his six-
> year-old brother, Casey, to the ground.
>
> "Whoa! What's going on?" I cried as I made my way to
> the scene of the crime.
>
> The boys were playing in the driveway with three of
> their neighborhood friends, and all five kids started talk-
> ing at once. Apparently, Patrick had discovered Casey
> using his skateboard without his permission. He had force-
> fully grabbed it away and yelled, "Dumbhead, who said
> you could use my skateboard?"
>
> "I just wanted to use it for a little bit," Casey had
> replied, tears welling up in his eyes.
>
> "Well, ask next time," Patrick had shouted, "so I can
> tell you no!" And with that, Patrick had pushed Casey to
> the asphalt. That's when I entered the scene.
>
> "Patrick, I can understand your being mad that Casey

1

borrowed your skateboard without asking," I said, "but you can't push him like that. Pushing is totally inappropriate."

"Well, he deserved it! He didn't borrow it—he stole it. He should have asked first!"

"Yes, he should have asked first. But still, we don't go pushing each other when one of us makes a mistake."

"He didn't make a mistake! He took it on purpose!" Patrick cried, pushing Casey to the ground one more time.

"That's it!" I said as I grabbed Patrick by the arm. "Up to your room until you are ready to act appropriately!"

"No way! Casey's the one who should go to his room for stealing my skateboard!"

"Patrick, I'll deal with your brother. Right now I need you to cool off."

Patrick stomped into the house and up to his bedroom. I followed him as far as the bottom of the stairs and heard his door slam.

I should have realized at that point that his volcano was still erupting, because I could hear the sound of furniture sliding across the hardwood floor upstairs. I didn't react, thinking that rearranging his room just might help him burn off some of his explosive energy. I went back to the project I was working on outside.

The next thing I knew, the kids playing in the driveway started screaming, "He's breaking the window!" I looked up and, sure enough, the south window of Patrick's room was shattered.

I ran into the house and up the stairs to find the bedroom door barricaded. I yelled; Patrick yelled. It wasn't a pretty scene. Finally I pushed my way into his room and asked what happened.

"You can't make me have a time out!" he screamed.

"Are you all right?"

"Yeah," he said more calmly.

I took him into my arms and held him, thinking the whole time: *What are we going to do?*

Can you identify with our friend Lisa? We can. We were such wonderful parents—and then we had a child. Those three little words, "It's a boy!" changed our lives forever. The doctor could have added, "It's a strong-willed boy!" But he didn't have to. In the following days and months, it was obvious to us that our son had a mind of his own.

Since this was our first child, we assumed that all kids come with strong wills—and to some extent that's true. Do you have a spirited, strong-willed child? If he or she is your only child, you probably think so. If you have more than one child, however, you know that difficult and spirited are a matter of degree. When it comes to children, there seems to be a continuum ranging from compliant on the one end through spirited, difficult, oppositional, and ending with explosive:

Compliant   Spirited   Difficult   Oppositional   Explosive

In this book we want to give you insights and ideas to encourage you on your parenting journey, whatever end of the scale your child is on—but especially if he or she tends to fall somewhere in the middle of the continuum. To help you determine where your child fits, check out the "Spirited Child Inventory" found on page 4. Rate each statement on a scale of one to ten, one being "Not my child," and ten being "Yep, that's definitely my kid!"

Now add up the score. If it's under fifty, you probably have a very compliant, cooperative child. And even though he or she would not be classified as "spirited" or "difficult," you will still find tips in this book that will make your job as a parent even more enjoyable. If your child's

Spirited Child Inventory

____When energy was given out, your child got an extra portion.

____The word *no* is considered a challenge, not an answer.

____Whatever your child is doing, he or she is very intense.

____Your child doesn't understand the concept of *adaptability*.

____Your child is a natural-born debater.

____Whatever the norm is for most children, your son or daughter is more.

____Your child resists schedules—as in bedtimes, meal-times, and routines.

____Your child gives a new meaning to the word *persistence*.

____Your child is sensitive to sounds, sights, textures, foods, and so on.

____Your child often loses his or her temper.

____Your child seems to try deliberately to annoy people.

____Your child often refuses to comply with your rules or requests.

score is between seventy and eighty, you most likely picked up this book because you recognize your little angel in the title. If your child scored even higher—well, we recommend that you find some other parents with similarly spirited children and develop a support system. You need it.

Just remember: If you're the parent of a spirited child, you're not alone! Here's what one friend wrote to us:

> I relate so well to Lisa's story of Patrick breaking the window and moving the furniture. The last two days have been one meltdown after another with our younger son, Kyle, who is nine. He is definitely a spirited child! He scored an 84 on your Spirited Child Inventory. Like Patrick, Kyle has often barricaded his bedroom door. He needs a lot of time to cool down.
>
> All the way to school on Tuesday, he was practically in tears, complaining that his older brother always gets his way. "You never get him in trouble," he cried. "I tell you all these bad things he does, but you never get him in trouble." His brother was sitting next to him in the car, and Kyle yelled at him, "You have an idiotic brain!" It seems that every statement Kyle makes deserves an exclamation mark.
>
> I think what bothers me the most is that Kyle hears rejection in whatever I say. He yelled the other day, "You never listen to me. Since you hate me, I hate you back!" So many times I just leave him alone and come back to him later, but even then, he still hears rejection. I'm afraid that I take the wind out of his sails. I want to reassure him then that I do love him, but he perceives rejection in

every comment. He cuts off his nose to spite his face—
daily. I pray so hard every day for peace. This is hard!

What Children Say—and What They Really Mean

What is it that frustrates you most about your spirited child? When
we asked this question in a survey of approximately two hundred parents
in both the United States and Europe, we discovered that children are
children all over the world. Spirited, difficult children challenge their
parents in similar ways, whether they live in Frankfurt, Germany, or
Knoxville, Tennessee. Here are some of the things parents told us:

> "My son bounds out of bed each morning and races
> through the day like a ten-ton truck. He's only eight years
> old. I shudder to think what he will be like as a teenager!"

> "I feel as if I'm always bribing my child or giving in
> because I just don't want to fight the battle. It takes too
> much energy to try to reason with her."

> "I don't know what to do when my child looks me right in
> the eye and says 'No!'"

> "My child is so intent on having things go his way—and
> when they don't, he explodes!"

> "When I discipline my son, he just looks at me and says, 'So?'"

Do any of these statements sound familiar? The interesting thing
we've discovered from our survey data (and from more than two
decades of work in the field of family education) is that spirited children not only have common characteristics and behaviors, they have
common needs. And what they often cry out to their parents—maybe

not in literal words, but in their actions—is this: "Mom, Dad, I need something specific from you to help me grow and mature as a person."

Of course, all children, even the most compliant ones, have similar needs; but spirited children often demand more of their parents' patience, understanding, leadership, and creativity in interpreting and meeting those needs. Spirited kids rarely verbalize their needs in a calm, direct way. Rather, they cry out in angry words or forceful actions—and it's up to their parents to "hear" what they're really saying.

If you can relate to our friends' stories about Patrick and Kyle or to any of the frustrations expressed by the parents above, this book is definitely for you. Our purpose in writing, however, is not to share a "perfect parenting plan" or give you "five simple steps" to parenting the spirited child. Rather, in the following chapters, we will present the eight most common cries you are likely to hear from your child as he or she grows up:

Cry #1: "Look at me!"

Cry #2: "Did I do good?"

Cry #3: "You're not listening!"

Cry #4: "I want to do it my way!"

Cry #5: "You can't make me!"

Cry #6: "I hate you!"

Cry #7: "I don't want to!"

Cry #8: "I am a big kid already!"

No doubt you've heard many, if not all, of these cries in your own house already. But did you know that each of these cries has a deeper meaning, one that your child doesn't quite know how to express? Our goal is to help you understand what your child *really* means when he or she cries out (or acts out) in one of these ways—then help you develop a winning strategy for meeting those needs. We want to equip you in your role as a parent so you can confidently guide your spirited child in the right direction toward maturity. Ultimately, we want to help you develop and maintain a healthy relationship with your son or daughter that will span a lifetime.

Why Me?

You may be wondering just how and why your child became such a challenge. In our survey, some parents told us they knew their children were spirited from day one. Others said that one day, quite suddenly, they realized their children were more in control than they were—and they didn't know how it happened. Whether your child was born spirited or grew into the role doesn't really matter. Your challenge now is to channel all that surplus energy, spirit, and determination in a positive way.

Who knows? You may be parenting the future scientist who will discover the cure for cancer! Don't laugh—many of the world's greatest leaders were strong-willed, spirited children. Did you know that Winston Churchill was a discipline problem? Or that Albert Einstein flunked math? Don't you just know their parents were frustrated!

"But why me?" you ask. The best answer is this: God chose you because he knew you were the parent your child would need. And he didn't make a mistake. *You have what it takes*. And whatever you lack in patience or wisdom or self-control, God will give you so you can see this job through.

If you feel fainthearted, we suggest that you get with other parents who have spirited children and work through this book together. One of the best survival tactics we found when we were raising our boys was to form our own parent support group. As we discovered, sometimes the best source of encouragement and information is other parents who are in the same boat. We came to believe this so strongly that we ended up developing a program called PEP Groups for Parents to help facilitate what the acronym stands for: "Parents Encouraging Parents."

Whether you work through this book alone, with your spouse, or with a supportive group of friends, remember this: Progress is more important than perfection. Unfortunately, many parents lose sight of this distinction. In our work and through our PEP Groups, we've met many moms and dads who were convinced that they didn't have what it takes to parent their spirited or difficult kids. They continually compared themselves with the Super Parents Model—you know, those perfect parents whose children are pleasant and cooperative and always remember to say "please" and "thank you." Parents who start each day with a smile because their children never irritate them or bring them to tears. Parents who know when and how to discipline—and always get the result they expected. (Actually, we've never met any Super Parents, but we understand they exist.)

We hope *you* are such a parent. But chances are you're more like us, not naturally patient, loving, or cheerful. Often tired. Occasionally ready to pull your hair out. We weren't Super Parents—just ask our kids who are now grown, married, and parents themselves.

Raising our three sons was definitely the most challenging and difficult job of our lives. We learned from experience that having spirited children definitely makes the process of parenting more intense and sometimes overwhelming. We made more than our share of mistakes. We also experienced some wonderful successes. Through it all, we worked hard to maintain healthy relationships with our sons.

Ultimately, we survived. That means you can too! We are living proof that it is entirely possible to be a parent of a spirited child and still maintain your sanity. (We'll give you some specific tips on how to do this in the last chapter.) Throughout this book we will share from our own experience and the experience of other parents who've raised strong-willed, spirited kids. We will also glean insights from parent education research and that ultimate parenting guide, the Bible.

Of course, this book is not intended to be a substitute for the professional, medical, or therapeutic assistance that may be needed in certain circumstances. But our prayer is that these pages will be a significant source of help and encouragement to you.

A Few Tips for the Road

Did you know that as a parent, you are a mirror for your child's emotions? When you're angry, your child will probably be angry. When you are tense, you can expect your child to be tense. When you are lighthearted, your child just may exhibit a better outlook on life. But how is it possible to be a positive and confident parent when your child is doing everything he or she can to make it hard for you?

There's no question that parenting is a demanding job—and all the more so if you have a spirited child. The hours are long, the pay is low, and affirmation? Don't hold your breath! The truth is, you are on one of the most difficult journeys you will ever take in your life. But it is also one of the most important and, ultimately, one of the most fulfilling. So as we get started, we want to give you a few tips to take on the road—things that we've learned through our work with parents and our own experience.

These first three are just for you:

- *Don't base your sense of self-worth on your child's performance.*
  If you do, you'll feel great on the days your child does well
  and terrible on days he or she makes a dumb decision.

- *Keep your sense of humor.* Don't take yourself so seriously! Laughter relieves tension and promotes good health. You'll have lots of good stories to repeat to your child when he or she is grown.

- *Take care of yourself.* You're human. That means you need sufficient sleep and a healthy diet. As one mother wrote to us, "It's difficult to maintain a calm demeanor when I'm tired. I feel as if I yell too much." Your child can literally sap you of all your energy and make you feel as if your only identity is his or her keeper. Save some of yourself to exercise, socialize, and be your own person.

These next four tips are for your relationship with your child:

- *Do what you can to promote mutual respect.* If you want your child to respect you, you need to show respect to your child.

- *Try to really get to know your child by planning one-on-one times.* Look for a few minutes every day when you can focus solely on him or her. Learn more about what makes your child unique. Seek to discover what brings your child real joy.

- *Limit your absolute noes.* For example, instead of saying, "Don't shout," say, "Use your inside voice."

- *Respond to the verbal and nonverbal cries of your child by following the principles we share in the following chapters.* To help you, we've divided each chapter into three main sections: "Understanding the Challenge," "Dealing with the Present," and "Taking Steps toward a Better Future." This third section includes practical ideas and activities that you can put into practice in your home starting *today*.

11

You're Going to Make It!

You may be wondering how Patrick's mom ended up handling the broken window episode. Here's what Lisa told us: "Amazingly, Patrick actually cooperated with the clean-up. He went with me to the glass and paint store. When he saw how much the bill was going to be, he agreed to pay for it out of his savings and allowance. But that's how it is with Patrick—a constant roller-coaster of emotions, never quite knowing what lies behind the next turn."

Several years have passed, and Patrick-the-Roller-Coaster is still surprising his parents. But Lisa says that she and her husband understand their spirited son's needs better now. They've discovered effective strategies for meeting those needs. And they're confident that, together, they're going to make it.

You're going to make it too! With God's help, you can and *will* become the confident parent your spirited child is desperately crying out for. Turn the page and let's begin to explore how.

CRY #1

"Look *at* Me!"

What it really means:
"Please understand me."

"Mom, I'd never want to make all A's!"

I (Claudia) stared at our son in disbelief. *How could anyone not want to get the best grades possible?* I thought. *Who is this kid? Did they switch babies on me in the hospital?*

I simply couldn't understand. I grew up in a home where academics were the key to success, not to mention a great self-concept. I can remember getting really upset when I got an A-minus. And now here I was, the mother of a kid who didn't want to get all A's.

Same kid, another day—and more evidence that an alien was living in our home, claiming to be our son. After much pleading on my part, he humored me by agreeing to go shopping with me to buy him a new shirt. Of course, we had different tastes. I chose the more conservative pinstriped shirt. He went for the paisley print.

OK, this is not a major issue, I thought. *I can compromise on this one.*

I took a deep breath. "Actually," I said, "that paisley print really looks good on you. Let's buy it."

His response: "Mom, why are you playing with my mind?"

We bought the shirt—the one he wanted—but guess who never

13

wore it? I just couldn't figure him out! And whenever I'd think that I was beginning to make progress, he would do a flip-flop.

My story is not an isolated one.

"What has happened to my little girl now that she's turned six?" asked a mom in one of our PEP Groups for Parents. "Five was manageable; but now that she's six, she's become a volcano ready to erupt if I cross her."

"I know what you mean," another parent said. "Just when I think I have almost figured out my son, he changes into someone totally different! Last year he loved school. This year he cries every morning and complains of a stomachache. I'm not sure what to do."

Understanding the Challenge

Can you identify with these parents? The trouble with trying to figure out spirited children is that by the time we do, they change! In fact, numerous parents tell us that, when it comes to their strong-willed or difficult kids, unpredictability is the norm. They also say that a big part of the stress they experience in the parenting process is that they never quite know when, where, or how their children are going to challenge them (or others). Change and challenge are the only two things some moms and dads feel they can count on!

But spirited kids do not set out deliberately to vex us. The reason their words and actions are often difficult or contrary is that they're trying to grab our attention. "Look at me!" they cry (although rarely in such direct terms). What these children really want—and what they really need—is our understanding.

Is It Just a Stage?

"Why is my eight-year-old so sensitive to criticism?"
"Why is my eleven-year-old so moody?"

14

To answer questions like these, an understanding of child development is crucial. You see, children are genetically programmed to achieve independence. And along the way, they pass through many developmental milestones. The more we know about these common ages and stages, the more we can support and encourage our children's physical, mental, emotional, social, and spiritual growth. This is especially true if our kids are strong-willed.

Take a look at the age-level characteristics we've listed in Appendix #1 at the back of the book. You'll discover the behaviors, attitudes, and moods that are typical of children at various ages, along with the level of maturity that can be expected at each stage. (For further study, an excellent resource we recommend is *Child Behavior: The Classic Childcare Manual from the Gesell Institute of Human Development* by Frances L. Ilg, M.D., Louise Bates Ames, Ph.D., and Sidney M. Baker, M.D.)

Physical development in children tends to follow a predictable order, although the timetable can vary from child to child. For example, one eight-month-old baby may begin crawling immediately after learning to sit up. Another may sit up, discover the pleasure of interacting with the world from a new perspective, and not get around to crawling for several weeks. Both babies are completely normal.

The timetable for emotional development can vary too. Emotional growth tends to occur in cycles, with periods of balance followed by periods that are more out of balance. Times of pleasant, agreeable behavior are followed by times of insecurity and disorder. These periods are evident whether a child is spirited or compliant; but with a spirited or difficult child, the cycles tend to swing from high to low with very little in between.

Many psychologists say that these normal emotional cycles are punctuated by two key periods of independence. The first comes between babyhood and childhood (the so-called terrible two's) and the second between childhood and adulthood (the onset of the teen years). If you're the parent of a spirited child, however, you can probably relate when we say that our strong-willed son expressed his independence not just at two and twelve, but at almost all of the ages and stages!

Don't get frazzled about the stage your child is in right now. By the time you've worked yourself into a total frenzy, your child will have done a flip-flop anyway!

As our children develop, the cycles of their lives are bound to include periods of rebellion, stress, and even obnoxious behavior. The good news is, if we know these times are coming, we can better accept them and handle them when they arrive. By being aware of developmental trends, we can recognize that the undesirable behavior we're witnessing is not true disobedi-ence or a sign of parental incompetence. Instead, it is behavior neces-sary to growth—an important step for our kids in developing independence physically, mentally, emotionally, socially, and spiritually.

Don't get frazzled about the stage your child is in right now. By the time you've worked yourself into a total frenzy, your child will have done a flip-flop anyway! The good news is that each stage marks progress; each stage is leading to maturity. And each stage is *temporary*. The more you know about child development, the better you'll be able to understand your child when he or she hits a rough spot. You'll know whether or not what you're seeing is normal—and if and when it's going to pass.

Understanding Your Child's Unique Personality

Not all kids, to look at them, are obviously spirited. A child with a seemingly laid-back, quiet personality can nevertheless have a will made of steel and exhibit a surprising level of spirited stubbornness. For this reason, in addition to understanding the normal stages of child development, it's important for us to understand our children's unique personalities.

One mother we know told us that every member of her family has a different personality type. In her home, as a result, "personality conflicts are hard to deal with," she says. "I'm a doer, my husband is a thinker, my son is a negotiator, and my daughter is a butterfly."

A *butterfly?* To understand what she means, you need to meet a few of the spirited kids we know. See if at least one of them isn't living at your house.

Suzie and Steven Sparkle

Suzie and Steven seem to just sparkle on everyone and everything around them. Outgoing and fun, they love to plan parties—and also direct them. Suzie and Steven are uninhibited and impulsive (a rather scary combination for their parents). Like butterflies, they flit from one thing to another. Their good intentions are sincere, but they lack follow-through. As a result, they leave behind toys, clothes, or unfinished projects as they move on like a ten-ton truck to something new.

At school Suzie and Steven try hard to keep their studies from interfering with their social lives. Teachers describe them as playful and borderline bossy and say that both kids need to concentrate more on their schoolwork.

Take-Charge Taylor and Tracy

Of all the kids we know, Taylor and Tracy are the most obviously spirited. They are organizers and natural-born leaders, and people always know when they're around. They're both decisive, and they have enough self-confidence for their whole family. They love to direct other people and can be either charming or obnoxious.

Strong-willed and hardworking, Taylor and Tracy can also be domineering and sometimes walk over other people (especially their parents). They consider their brother or sister's closet their own and don't hesitate to borrow whatever they need. Patience and sympathy are definitely not their strongest attributes. Teachers enjoy their quick minds but say the classroom could do just fine without their sarcasm.

Laid-Back Lucas and Lindsey

Lucas and Lindsey are the last kids you might think of as spirited. But they are—they just exhibit their strong wills in more pleasant ways than, say, Taylor and Tracy. Their sense of humor helps to keep things light. Lucas and Lindsey are easy-going, calm, and rarely get angry—that is, until you cross them or tell them, "No, absolutely not!" They often seem to be in a world of their own (and as our son—a Lucas and Lindsey type—once said, "I like it in here!").

Life for Lucas and Lindsey is a pleasant, unexciting experience. Slowness and lack of motivation are their greatest liabilities. But when they do get motivated by a personal goal, they dig their heels in and accomplish much. They tend to be underachievers at school and can drive teachers (and parents) crazy.

Roller-Coaster Russell and Rachel

Russell and Rachel are spirited too; they're just more introverted. They're creative, and sometimes they amaze people with their insights—

like, "Mom, are you trying to manipulate me?" Woe to their parents when these two become negative and introspective!

While the sparklers, Steven and Suzie, openly express their feelings, Russell and Rachel feel deeply but don't always express their emotions in an outward way. They tend to ride a feelings roller coaster—high then low, up then down. They can easily convince themselves that they are unloved and that their brother or sister is the family favorite.

Russell and Rachel are ultra-responsible kids. Their teachers are quick to say what good students they are but that they shouldn't take life so seriously.

What's Your Combination?

No doubt you recognize some of the characteristics we've just described in your own spirited child. In our PEP Groups for Parents program, we use the Basic Personality Chart on page 20 to help parents better understand their children. Obviously such a simple grid doesn't allow for in-depth analysis, but it does help identify a child's particular tendencies.

Can you identify your child's basic personality from this chart? Actually, most children are a combination of types, with one type that is dominant—for example, 60 percent Take-Charge and 40 percent Roller-Coaster, or 70 percent Sparkle and 30 percent Laid-Back. Of course, every personality has its attractive and unattractive qualities. With the positive comes the negative—and vice versa. When we know our children's basic personality traits, we can be realistic in our expectations of them, concentrating on playing up their strengths and encouraging them to overcome their weaknesses.

Basic Personality Chart [1]

Sparkler	Take-Charge	Roller-Coaster	Laid-Back
Strengths	*Strengths*	*Strengths*	*Strengths*
Friendly	Motivated	Deep thinker	Calm
Responsible	Determined	Sensitive	Cool
Warm	Strong-willed	Analytical	Peace-loving
Talkative	Confident	Creative	Dependable
Generous	Bold	Idealistic	Practical
Impulsive	Daring	Perfectionist	Adaptable
Charming	Energetic	Self-sacrificing	Efficient
Sympathetic	Practical	Genuine	Good-natured
Tender	Quick-thinking	Orderly	Stabilizing
Impressionable	Decisive	Faithful	Impartial
Fun	Persistent	Self-disciplined	Diplomatic
	Faithful	Thorough	Witty
Weaknesses	*Weaknesses*	*Weaknesses*	*Weaknesses*
Undisciplined	Domineering	Moody, self-centered	Slow
Weak-willed	Stubborn	Sad	Lazy
Self-indulgent	Rebellious	Negative	Easily stagnated
Unreliable	Hot-tempered	Pessimistic	Indifferent
Changeable	Reckless	Haughty	Passive
Unpredictable	Violent	Easily offended	Apathetic
Restless	Sarcastic	Suspicious	Detached
Unproductive	Haughty	Vengeful	Dislikes inconvenience
Disorganized	Crafty	Unforgiving	Self-righteous
Shallow	Vengeful	Impractical	Proud
Fickle	Hard to please	Seldom satisfied	Arrogant
Unfocused	Unsympathetic		Scornful

Understanding Your Child's Life Orientation

Another way we can better understand our children is to look at the following two continuums dealing with life orientation—that is, how our kids relate to life in general and to other people in particular.

Reactive vs. Adaptive

Reactive   **Adaptive**

All of us fall somewhere on this continuum in our general orientation toward life. We tend to either react or adapt to the situations and circumstances we find ourselves in. Where would you place your child on this scale? Does he or she tend to be more reactive or more adaptive?

Think back to when your spirited child was a baby. How did he or she react to noise? As a newborn, did your child become unsettled every time you ran the vacuum, or did the roar put your little one to sleep? Did it matter if the lights were on or off? As a toddler, did your child always get jumpy at the sound of the neighbor's lawn mower? Is he or she able to tune out the world while glued to the television, even though the phone is ringing, the food processor is running, and the dog is barking?

How does your child react to a schedule change? Again, think back. When a vacation required riding in a car for long hours, did your baby keep to a normal sleep pattern, or did every rest stop upset the schedule? At seven or eight, was your child peacefully entertained with solitary games and storybooks, or did he or she wiggle around a lot and ask, "Are we there yet?"

Reactive children make us very much aware when they are discontent with their environment. We might describe them as busy, active, transparent, high-strung, strong-willed, aggressive, difficult, spirited, activity-oriented, and born leaders. Adaptive children, on the other

21

hand, can tune out the world; they tend to be easygoing, laid-back, flexible, calm, and passive. Adaptive children may seem lazy, slow, and compliant, but they are also very affectionate, like to cuddle, and have a good sense of humor.

Most children fall somewhere between the two extremes—not always reactive *or* adaptive. One child may adapt really well to moving to a new home but struggle to adapt in other areas. Another child, usually very adaptive, may react more when he or she is sick or experiencing stress at school. As we might expect, spirited, difficult children tend to be more reactive than adaptive in their orientation to life.

Public vs. Private

Public		**Private**

Everyone falls somewhere on this continuum, too, which has to do with the way we relate to people. Where is your child on this scale? Is your child a very public person, or does he or she tend to be more private?

As a baby, did your child get fussy in the church nursery, sensing the hustle and bustle of activity, or did he or she enjoy being passed around from one admiring fan to another? As a toddler, did your child like going to the park with you for a quiet afternoon of playing alone on the swings or prefer the hustle and bustle of a shopping mall filled with people? Is your child the shining star at family gatherings, or does he or she stay glued to your side, uncomfortable around all the strangers? Does your child enjoy noise and activity or want everything quiet?

If our children are very public individuals, they are probably outgoing, fun, and people-oriented. They love groups and group activities and are always on the go. They are high achievers, but they're also frequently over-committed, disorganized, and forgetful. Children who are more private, by contrast, enjoy being alone; they resist group activities and usually have rich inner lives. They tend to be creative, artistic, introverted, introspective, melancholy, content, musical, and good listeners. They have sensitive natures and like personal space. They may go up and down emotionally.

On this continuum, spirited children do not necessarily lean more to one side than the other. Difficult, strong-willed kids can be people-oriented; they can also be very private by nature. As we saw in our discussion of personality traits, not all spirited children are extroverts.

Could My Child Be ADHD?

Sometimes parents wonder, *Could my child's difficult behavior be attributed to something more than personality and life orientation? Could there be something medically wrong with my child?* In 1987 the term "Attention Deficit Hyperactivity Disorder" (ADHD) was introduced in psychology and education circles. It soon became an umbrella label for a range of behaviors characterized by distractibility or inattention, hyperactivity, and impulsiveness.

If you are often bewildered and frustrated by your child's behavior and by your inability to control or understand your child, he or she may be showing signs of ADHD. Ask yourself the following questions:[2]

- Does your child fidget with his or her hands or feet?
- Does your child squirm when sitting in a seat?
- Do you have trouble keeping your child's attention?
- Is your child easily distracted by any outside stimulus?
- Does your child have difficulty waiting his or her turn in games or group situations?

- Does your son or daughter sometimes blurt out answers to questions in class before the question is even completed?
- Does your child have difficulty following through on instructions from other people?
- Does your child have difficulty sustaining attention, often shifting from one activity to another?
- Does your child find it hard to just play quietly?
- Does your child talk excessively or interrupt and intrude on others?
- Does your child not seem to listen to what is being said to him or her?
- Does your child often lose things necessary for a task or activity?
- Does your son or daughter often engage in physical or dangerous activities without considering the consequences?

If you answered "yes" to most of these questions, we encourage you to seek advice and help from a knowledgeable professional. Real ADHD is difficult to diagnose (and even more difficult for parents to cope with). More boys are diagnosed with ADHD than girls. But all behavioral problems are *not* ADHD; a good pediatrician, educator, or child psychologist can help you make that determination and develop an appropriate course of action.

Understanding Yourself

There's one more key to really knowing and understanding our children, and that's knowing *ourselves*. We need to understand how our unique personalities and parenting styles affect the way we relate to our children. Think about this: If you have more than one child, do you tend to get angry and react more toward one than another? Some parents find that they react more to the child who is the most *different* from them, while others get angry at the one who's most *like* them. (Sometimes there's nothing worse than seeing your faults lived out in your child's behavior!)

Take another look at the Basic Personality Chart on page 19 and try to identify your own strengths and weaknesses. Are you a Take-Charge kind of parent? If so, you may have a tendency to be too controlling with your child. Are you more Laid-Back? You could err on the side of being too passive or permissive. By assessing your temperament, you can be as alert to your own weaknesses as you are to your child's, and you can work to overcome them.

Now turn to Appendix #2, "What Kind of Parent Are You?" Answer the questions to determine whether you're reactive or adaptive, public or private in your orientation to life and relationships. When you understand yourself *and* your child, you can parent with greater confidence—and a confident parent is something every spirited child cries out for.

Dealing with the Present

Sometimes it seems that no matter what we do, our children keep pushing all the wrong buttons at all of the wrong times. It's so easy for us to become discouraged and feel as if we've failed as a parent! But giving in to such feelings does nothing to answer that underlying, unspoken cry of, "Please understand me!" Rather, we can only begin to answer that cry when we acknowledge and understand our own feelings about being the parent of a spirited child.

Facing Your Own Feelings and Fears

In our work with parents over the years, we have observed three emotions that are common to most moms and dads—and especially those who have spirited children: guilt, shame, and anger. Let's examine each one of these.

Feelings of Guilt

When asked on a morning talk show, "What is the one thing parents do wrong most often?" a well-known child psychologist answered, "They feel guilty." Guilt is a contagious disease that we often inherit from our own parents. It is developed out of a false assumption: that being a "good" parent means having happy children and a harmonious home. As a result, when we have a child who is not happy and who constantly causes discord in the family, we naturally assume that we're not "good" parents.

Are you harboring any parental guilt? Did you expect to have perfect kids—and now you feel guilty because they're less than perfect? It's time to let the guilt go and get on with the challenging job of parenting. Think about this: God is the perfect parent, yet throughout the Bible we read stories about his children rebelling and doing dumb things. Why should we expect perfection from *our* kids?

Feelings of Shame

Show me a parent who, at some time or another, has not felt shame because of something a child said or did. You can't, because there aren't any! Children are great at embarrassing their parents—in little ways and in big ways. Imagine the deep shame parents feel when their child is convicted of theft or murder or rape, or when the child chooses a lifestyle that is in total contradiction to their deepest beliefs. Hopefully most of us will never experience shame at such a level. But spirited kids in particular are good at coming up with all kinds of little, daily "shamers"—like returning from the mall with a weird hairstyle or refusing to take a bath for weeks on end or shouting out in the middle of the grocery store, "Mommy, I hate you. You're mean!"

If you are aware that you have feelings of shame, stop and ask yourself these questions:

- Are you comparing your child with other children who are more compliant?
- Are you caring too much about what others think of your parenting skills?
- Are you expecting adult maturity from your spirited, non-compliant child?
- Are you basing your own self-worth on your son or daughter's unpredictable behavior?

It's time to cut yourself a little slack and put things in perspective. The challenge of parenting a spirited child is difficult enough without your beating up on yourself. Instead, you should pat yourself on the back! You're a *good enough* parent—after all, aren't you reading this book so you can better understand and meet your child's needs? Your son or daughter is lucky to have a parent who cares that much!

Feelings of Anger

One of the greatest barriers to a healthy parent-child relationship is anger—whether it's overt, with lots of yelling and shouting, or more inward and hidden. Stuffing anger, however, can be dangerous; people who don't deal with their anger often become bitter and can even become physically sick.

Anger is actually a secondary emotion. It tends to be a reaction to either fear or frustration, two emotions that are very familiar to parents of difficult or spirited children. The fact is (and we know, because we experienced it in our own home), strong-willed kids are good at generating angry feelings. Dealing with those feelings in a positive way is the key to a healthy parent-child relationship. And the more we learn about processing our own anger, the better we are at helping our children deal with theirs.

But our kids are not the only ones we are angry with sometimes. We can also be angry with God, who created them and gave them to us. Have you ever thought to yourself that your difficult child was a "punishment" from God? (Be honest!) If so, let us reassure you: God is not punishing you by giving you a difficult child to bring you frequent anguish. While you probably wouldn't have volunteered to be the parent of a spirited child, you can be certain that God chose your son or daughter to help train you to become more like Christ. *This is the right child for you.* He or she is God's perfect catalyst to bring you the opportunities you need to develop godly character and greater compassion for others.

Practicing Acceptance and Forgiveness

"It's hard to thank God for a difficult child," one parent told us. "It's easier to be angry with God and angry with my child. But I know that if left unchecked, my anger can lead me to become bitter. I don't want to go down that path, so I try to focus on the thought, *God can give me the patience and wisdom and self-control that I need.* Because like all parents of difficult children, I need lots of all three!

"I try to remember that as the parent, it's important for me to model acceptance and forgiveness, even during the most difficult times. Otherwise, how will my child ever learn to accept and forgive others—and himself?"

As this mother recognized, building positive relationships with our children involves accepting them—even if their God-given personalities rub us the wrong way sometimes. One of the most wonderful things we have learned in life is that God loves us unconditionally. His love does not depend on our being perfect parents and making all the right decisions. God loves and accepts us just as we are, no strings attached. This total, unconditional love motivates us, not only to be all that God wants us to be, but also to love and accept our children in the same way—no matter how difficult or strong-willed they are. Our acceptance of them, like God's acceptance of us, encourages them to grow and become all that they can be. Ultimately, then, God can use their energy and determination to honor Him.

> *Let's face it. Parenting a difficult, strong-willed child often leaves us little or no time to relax or regroup. We overreact out of sheer exhaustion.*

Being a Model of Forgiveness

It's easy for parents to get stuck in negative patterns of responding to their children. As one mom said, "After my buttons have been pushed numerous times and in numerous ways, it's hard to be positive. Before I know it, I've overreacted!"

Most parents of spirited children *do* overreact at times, not out of faulty parenting skills, but rather because the numerous challenges of the day put them on edge emotionally. Let's face it. Parenting a difficult, strong-willed child often leaves us little or no time to relax or regroup. We overreact out of shear exhaustion. The question is, what do we do after we've gone "over the top"?

The answer is important because spirited children have a tendency to overreact to situations and stimuli. They need to be able to look to us for a model of how to respond at such times. In our home we found that the best thing to do was to take time to gather ourselves emotionally and then go to our son, apologize, and ask for forgiveness. We called this process "log removal," based on a principle found in Matthew 7:3–5: "And why worry about a speck in your friend's eye when you have a log in your own?…Hypocrite! First get rid of the log from your own eye; then perhaps you will see well enough to deal with the speck in your friend's eye" (NLT).

Changing Our Responses

To help you identify your negative or inappropriate reactions and begin to change them to more positive ones, make a chart with three columns. In the first column, list your child's difficult or irritating behaviors. (Don't show this page to your child.) In the second column, write the negative response you typically have to each behavior. For example, let's say your child has a terrible time getting up in the morning. What is your response? Do you yell, scream, nag, and threaten? How could you handle this situation differently in the future? *That's* what you write in the third column. Perhaps you could buy your child an alarm clock and explain that he or she is now responsible for getting up on time in the morning. Then you could spell out what the specific consequences will be if your son or daughter continues to oversleep—for example, no TV that day, or going to bed thirty minutes earlier that night.

Or let's say your child's difficult behavior is bickering with his or her siblings. Your standard—but inappropriate—response might be to yell at the kids to make them stop fighting. A better response, however, would be to recognize that it's *their* problem and let them work it out (as long as they don't physically hurt each other). You also could encourage them to verbally communicate their feelings.

We should add one caveat here. Spirited children *do* have a tendency to overwhelm or overpower their siblings at times. In some cases it may be appropriate for you to step in, even if they're not yet throwing punches. Just try not to impose a solution. Instead, coach them in the process of solving the problem. Ask questions that help them come up with possible solutions, and help them think through the ramifications of each one. You may see the pitfall of the course of action they choose, but resist the urge to interfere unless their decision will lead to additional problems for others. Help them learn from their mistakes. (To understand more about the unique dynamics of sibling relationships, we recommend the book *Siblings without Rivalry: How to Help your Children Live Together So You Can Live Too* by Adele Faber and Elaine Mazlish.)

Be Thankful for Positive Qualities

Does your spirited child try hard to perform well in school? Control his or her temper? Take a few moments and make a list of all your child's positive actions and attitudes. Now take a few moments more to be thankful for each one of them.

Philippians 4:8 says, "Finally, brothers, whatever is true, whatever is noble, whatever is right, whatever is pure, whatever is lovely, whatever is admirable—if anything is excellent or praiseworthy—think about such things." Unfortunately, it's easy for us to forget this verse and dwell instead on our kids' deficiencies, flaws, and faults. But concentrating on the negative—especially during the turbulent preadolescent years— can make our children feel unloved, unappreciated, and devalued. If what they hear consistently from us are statements of disapproval and discouragement, we may just drive them out of our homes and into the arms of whatever "in" peer group is willing to accept them as they are.

Our challenge to you is to dwell on your child's positive qualities—and be willing to apologize to your child when you blow it and over-react. That will help clear the air so you can accept your child with no strings attached and, in the future, concentrate on the positive that you see in his or her life.

Taking Steps toward a Better Future

Understanding your spirited child is, admittedly, not an easy task. But there are a number of concrete, practical activities you can do to get to know your child better. Here are some to try:

Plan Just-You-and-Me Times

All children need focused, personal time with their parents. One way to ensure that you spend good one-on-one time with your child is to start a tradition of Just-You-and-Me times. A Just-You-and-Me activity could be as simple as ten minutes of playing on the floor with your toddler. It could be a planned afternoon outing with your ten-year-old to the local children's museum. Be intentional and plan to have focused time with each child, one on one, as often as is practical for you. (Hint: Younger children love to talk about and make plans for Just-You-and-Me activities. Older children and preteens need Just-You-and-Me times, too, but smart parents don't call it that!)

Use Open-Ended Statements

A good way to get your child to open up and talk to you is to use open-ended statements. Here are some to start with:

- The funniest thing that ever happened to me was....
- If I had a million dollars, I would....
- If I could visit anywhere in the world, I would go to....
- The one thing I like the most about me is....
- The one thing I like the most about you is....
- If I could change one thing about our family, it would be....

Let your child suggest some statements for you to fill in too.

Make "Positive Sandwiches"

Many times we need to correct or redirect our spirited children, but we don't want to come across as always being negative. Difficult, spirited children usually come with heightened negative feelings as it is. If you must express something negative, try to do it in a positive way—and teach your child to do the same.

When our kids were growing up, we made "positive sandwiches." We tried to "sandwich" a negative statement between two positive statements. How does this work? You might say, for example, "I really appreciate your attempt to clean your room, but stuffing clothes under the bed is unacceptable. On the other hand, I notice that your desk is well organized. Now what can you do about the clothes?" Or you might coach your child to say, "Jay let me play with his Legos, but he called me a nerd. The good news is he didn't hit me."

Write Notes

Writing a note to your son or daughter not only sends a positive message, it may actually help your child learn to better express his or her own feelings. Leave little notes where you know your child will find them. Write things such as, "Your humor is a bright light in our family!" Or, "Your cooperation this morning sure made breakfast more pleasant! Keep it up!"

Watch for an Opening

Be on the lookout for times when your child seems open to talking with you. Be ready with impromptu activities to facilitate conversation. For example:

- Take a cookie break. Don't just bake the cookies—sit down and eat them together!
- Listen to music or watch a TV program of his or her choice.
- Surf some interesting, child-friendly sites on the Internet together.
- Do a craft together. Make a collage of common items from your kitchen by gluing cereal pieces, macaroni, noodles, beans, or other small items to a sheet of poster board.

Do the Dinnertime Shuffle

Ask every member of the family to sit in someone else's place at the dinner table—and tell them to act like the person whose place they're sitting in!

Plan a Family Appreciation Night

Get the family together and give each member a three by five index card and a pencil. Have them write down one thing they appreciate about each person in the family. (Oral answers are fine for younger children who can't write yet.) Then take turns sharing your insights with each other. Or ask each person to write an answer to one of the following questions:

- What is the greatest strength I bring to our family?
- What is the one thing I like best about our family?

You'll enjoy hearing the positive answers. Be prepared to laugh off the silly or sarcastic ones!

Getting Started Today

Our children come to us in such unique packages, each one radically different from the next. As parents, we need to make every effort to understand each child and appreciate his or her God-given uniqueness— even when that uniqueness includes a strong will and a spirit that's hard to keep in check some days. At the same time, we need to remember that *we're* the adults in the relationship; we're the ones who need to set the limits, make the difficult decisions, and take the lead in turning negative situations into positive ones for us and our kids.

Whatever the current state of your relationship with your spirited child, a better relationship can start today! As you begin to understand, to love, to forgive, and to accept your child as a special individual placed in your life by a loving, all-knowing God, you will find yourself responding to him or her in more positive and effective ways. And the response you'll get back will make it all worthwhile.

"Did I *do* Good?"

What it really means:
"Encourage me. Look for the positive."

Nine-year-old Hunter had a stubborn streak. Always adamant that things go his way, he often tired out his parents and siblings with his frequent complaining and rigid demands. His stubborn persistence was not all negative, however. The positive side of this trait became apparent to his dad one cold November afternoon when the two decided to go on a hike in the woods.

Checking the large map on the sign at the trailhead, Hunter and his dad saw that several trails were available to them. Most were fairly long, meaning they would have to turn around and retrace their steps at some point to get back to the trailhead before dark. One route that passed near the lake, however, was shorter and circled back around to their starting point. It seemed to be just the right distance for the amount of daylight they had left. This circular trail was not shown on a separate winter map that Hunter's dad had obtained sometime earlier; but since the trailhead sign showed the route quite clearly, the two set out with confidence.

Before long they discovered why this particular trail wasn't on the winter map. As they approached the lake, the path became very icy, and the journey became difficult—even dangerous in some places. The sun was setting rapidly, and Hunter's dad considered turning around.

But since they'd passed the halfway mark, he figured that completing the circle was the shorter distance. They continued to push ahead along the treacherous path.

It was at that point that Hunter's stubbornness became a huge asset. His will rose up with a determination and perseverance that would not be swayed. Another child might have looked at the sky and the ice and the distance still to go and given up, making the rest of the journey all the more difficult. But Hunter was as inflexible as ever—and this time, his father was thankful for it!

When they finally got home that evening, tired but exhilarated, Hunter and his dad told the story of their adventure. Hunter's mom flinched when she heard about the dangers the two had encountered; but when she saw the glow on her son's face as her husband recounted in detail how well Hunter had responded to the challenge, she couldn't help but smile.

Years have passed since that day in the woods. Even now Hunter and his dad tell their hiking story to whoever will listen—always emphasizing how Hunter's perseverance and determination won the day.

Do you have a son or daughter as persistent and stubborn as Hunter? Do you ever celebrate that stubbornness as a strength—or do you see it only as a liability? Your answer is important, because your attitude communicates volumes. Children look to their parents for approval. They learn who they are by how Mom and Dad label them. Helping your spirited or difficult child develop a favorable and resilient self-concept is one of the major challenges you face as a parent.

Understanding the Challenge

When asked to write three conclusions for the sentence beginning, "I am…" one child wrote, "I am ugly. I am not very smart. I am sad."

Another wrote, "I am a good painter. I am funny. I am bright." What do you think *your* child would write?

Perhaps the more important question is, What would *you* write about your spirited child? Would you write, "My child is demanding" or "My child is persistent"? Would you write, "My child is whiny" or "My child is expressive"? "My child is stubborn" or "My child is focused and not easily swayed"?

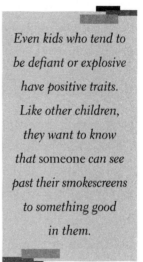

Even kids who tend to be defiant or explosive have positive traits. Like other children, they want to know that someone can see past their smokescreens to something good in them.

If you tend to think about your child in negative terms, it's time to think again. Negative terms lead to negative labels. And negative labels lead to negative behavior. If you consistently refer to your strong-willed child as "the difficult one," he or she will only become more difficult! That's why this chapter on accentuating and encouraging the positive qualities in our children is so vital. Even kids who tend to be defiant or explosive have positive traits. Like other children, they want to know that *someone* can see past their smokescreens to something good in them. And while parenting a noncompliant child is definitely more challenging than parenting a more adaptable child, it doesn't have to be a negative experience—especially if we're willing to make the effort to focus on the positive.

Granted, for most of us, maintaining a positive focus is not an easy task. Our children's negative behaviors tend to cast a long shadow over the positive ones. And unfortunately, many well-meaning relatives and friends only make matters worse.

One woman we know, Sandra, always dreads her mother's visits. One of Sandra's daughters, Tabitha, is strong-willed, and from the moment Grandma walks in the door until she leaves, she nags Sandra incessantly about the way Tabitha is (or isn't) disciplined. She lavishes attention and praise on Tabitha's younger, more compliant sister; but toward Tabitha, she is cool and distant. Tabitha senses her grandmother's disapproval, of course, and is stiff and unfriendly in return. She then acts out to get her mother's attention, fueling her grandmother's negative view of her even more. Poor Sandra feels caught in the middle.

When You Don't Like Your Child

As we discussed in the last chapter, parents of spirited children often struggle with feelings of guilt, shame, and anger. Sometimes they feel these things because they just don't *like* their children. Don't misunderstand; we're not suggesting that they don't *love* their children unconditionally. Of course they do. Rather, we're acknowledging the fact that many parents have times when their children act up so much that, for the moment, they really don't like being around them! The truth is, we would have to be angels to enjoy children when they're deliberately bucking us and draining us emotionally by their words or behavior. Those "I don't think I like you" feelings are natural. It's what we do with them that's key.

Turning Negatives into Positives

Growing up, one of our sons was a melancholy, negative kid—the kind who always sees the glass as half empty instead of half full. As far as he was concerned, everyone was against him. Once he walked into the kitchen and said, "Mom, stop nagging me."

I (Claudia) was shocked. I hadn't said a word, and I told him so. "I know, Mom," he responded, "but it's your nonverbal nagging that I hate!"

Believe me, it wasn't easy to redefine his hypersensitivity as a positive trait, but I gave it my best effort. Over time I saw his sensitive nature become something more positive, particularly when he started playing the guitar and writing songs that expressed deep, heartfelt emotions—and they weren't always negative ones! Years later at college, he joined a music group, and it became a great outlet for him to express his feelings, both positive and negative.

Now as an adult, he's a Web page designer—a profession in which sensitivity and creativity are great assets. And we, his parents, are reaping some of the benefits: He designed, launched, and currently monitors our Web site. Does he still get negative sometimes? Yes, but he has matured to the point that he can manage it. Does he still react to nonverbal messages and misinterpret us at times? Yes, but on balance, we see his sensitivity as far more of an asset now than a liability.

We're convinced that our early efforts to see the positive sides of our son's negative traits helped him to see *himself* in a more positive light—and, over time, the positives began to overshadow the negatives. "Self-fulfilling prophecies" work both ways, you know. When we begin to see our children in terms of their positive traits rather than their negative ones, they start to become what we see. The "extreme" is let out of their behavior, like air out of a balloon, and our relationships with them become increasingly more positive.

Reframing Extreme Terms

Take a few minutes to look back through the last chapter and list all the descriptive words you find that describe your spirited child. Now consider how many of those terms have negative connotations. Can you think of a way to turn those negatives around and put each facet of your child's personality in a positive light? For instance, can you look at your

41

child's up-and-down, melancholy personality as sensitivity? Can the term *whininess* be reframed to *very expressive*? If your child's extreme behavior was modified somewhat, could it have a positive side?

In a University of Nebraska study of three thousand families, the following extreme behaviors were "reframed" and given more positive terms.[1] Which ones apply to your child? Can you make your own list?

Reframing Extreme Behaviors	
Extreme	Reframed
Wastes money	Generous
Talks too much	Likes to share with others
Bossy	A leader
Messy, into things	Curious
Won't follow rules	Creative, innovative
Too picky	Attends to details
Interfering, nosey	Interested, concerned
Domineering	Has strong opinions
Stubborn	Determined
Fragmented	Multifaceted, talented
Shy, timid	Self-contained
Meek	Gentle, mild
Gossipy	Articulate

Once a parent in one of our PEP Groups asked, "Isn't this just semantics? My kid is negative. Why should I sugar coat it and say he's analytical?"

That's a good question, and it deserves a good answer. As we said in the last chapter, we are mirrors for our children. How our children see themselves is greatly influenced by how they think *we* see him. When we view them negatively, that negativity comes through in our verbal and nonverbal communication—and they hear us loud and clear. If we think they are a certain way, *they* think they are a certain way. If we think they can't do something, *they* think they can't do something—and that means they probably never will do it. On the other hand, when we look at our children through a more positive filter, we give more positive feedback; we smile more; we're more pleasant to be around; we listen more attentively; we're more encouraging. We expect more from them, and they expect more from themselves. It's that simple.

The eighteenth-century poet Johann Wolfgang Goethe once said that if you treat a person as he is, he'll stay that same person; but if you treat him as if he were the bigger and better person he can become, he will become that bigger and better person. This is a great principle that can help us stay focused on the fact that our children's difficult traits today can become positive attributes in the future. Just think: Your child may be bossy now, but someday he may be president of the company!

> If we want our children to mature into successful, productive adults, we need to do everything we can to turn the negative images we have of them into potentially positive ones.

In our home we used to say that our most spirited son would make an impact on this world—one way or the other. We tried hard to picture his impact as a positive one. Happily, he didn't disappoint us. He is now a successful attorney, but you can be sure he cut his first legal teeth arguing his cases with us.

If we want our children to mature into successful, productive adults, we need to do everything we can to turn the negative images we have of them into potentially positive ones. And we need to help them understand that by learning to modify their negative behavior, they can turn those negatives into wonderful positives that will serve them (and others) well in the future.

The Story of Jack

We met Jack when we hired him to build some bookcases in our home. Unfortunately, one bookcase was never completed. Jack had designed it with a library ladder; but after building the shelves, he stopped and never built the ladder to go with it. He just dropped the job.

We were puzzled about his behavior until we realized that he had designed the ladder incorrectly. Apparently Jack couldn't handle failure, and rather than admit he'd made a mistake and work to correct it, he simply quit the job. We were disappointed; but when we remembered an earlier conversation we'd had with him, we understood his actions.

While working on the bookcases, he'd told us about his strained relationship with his father. This was his story:

> My dad never encouraged me. While I was growing up, he kept telling me how dumb I was and how smart my older brother was. In school, teachers just passed me to the next grade. I was convinced I couldn't learn, so I didn't even try.
>
> I was a loner, and since my bedroom was in the attic, I would go there and get away from my family. From my earliest memory, I loved airplanes and always wanted to be a pilot. I spent hours and hours in my room building model airplanes. But I still remember my dad telling me, "Jack, you'll never be a pilot. You're just not smart enough. The only planes you will fly are in your dreams."
>
> When I was old enough to leave home, I joined the air force. I figured if I was too dumb to fly, at least I could learn how to work on the planes.

Fortunately, Jack married a girl who really believed in him and encouraged him to give life a chance. So while he was still in the air

44

force, Jack went back to school and then to officers training. Eventually he became a pilot. When he left the military, he flew for a major airline until he retired. Now he does part-time carpentry work.

But the scars from his dad's negativity still remain. As a fifty-five-year-old man, Jack still struggles with a low opinion of himself—an opinion he developed from all those years spent looking at himself through his dad's mirror. When he was working in our home, he seemed to be in need of our constant approval and praise. It was as if there were a little boy inside of him asking, "Did I do good?" Many times we said to ourselves that Jack wanted our affirmation more than the money we were paying him for building the bookcases.

How do you look at your son or daughter? Through negative glasses or positive ones? What does your child see when he or she looks in *your* mirror? Remember, the way that you view and relate to your child today will have a great impact on how well he or she functions later as an adult. Jack's dad handicapped his son for life. You can choose instead to offer encouragement and give your child a leg up on the future. It's your choice.

Dealing with the Present

A mother once asked, "How can I focus on the positive when my 'analytical' and 'expressive' kid has been in 'time out' four times before lunch? He's driving me crazy!"

We never said it would be easy! But it's definitely *easier* when we stop and take time to consider God's perspective on our spirited children. After all, he's the one who made them exactly the way they are. Psalm 139:13–16 is a wonderful passage that tells us how God looks at our kids. It's a great scripture for parents—and a great one to share with our children, whatever their ages. The Living Bible paraphrases it this way:

> You made all the delicate, inner parts of my body, and knit them together in my mother's womb. Thank you for making me so wonderfully complex! It is amazing to think about. Your workmanship is marvelous—and how well I know it. You were there while I was being formed in utter seclusion! You saw me before I was born and scheduled each day of my life before I began to breathe. Every day was recorded in your Book!

Why not read this scripture to your child today, emphasizing the words "wonderfully complex," "marvelous," and "amazing"? Explain that this is God's perspective on his or her appearance, abilities, intelligence, and temperament—including the strong-willed, spirited parts. Then, the next time you get frustrated, stop and remember that God wired your child this way on purpose. Thank him that he has given your child everything that he or she needs to grow up and be all that God intends.

Essentials of Encouragement

The Bible says that we should "encourage one another and build each other up" (1 Thess. 5:11). Encouragement is an important element of success in life. In a leadership class for business professionals, James Kouzes and Barry Posner, authors of *Encouraging the Heart: A Leader's Guide to Rewarding and Recognizing Others*, asked participants, "When you get encouragement, does it help you perform at a higher level?" Amazingly, 98 percent said yes, and only 2 percent said no! Apparently, almost everyone does better when they receive words of encouragement—and we think that's especially true of children. In fact, Kouzes and Posner identified seven essentials of effective encouragement that we've adapted for parents who want to encourage their kids:[2]

1. *Set clear standards.* Be certain your child knows what is expected of him or her.

2. *Expect the best.* Communicate that you believe in your child and that he or she can do what is expected.

3. *Pay attention.* Catch your child doing things well.

4. *Personalize recognition.* Let your son or daughter know specifically what you appreciate and why.

5. *Tell the story.* Don't be afraid to brag about what your child does right.

6. *Celebrate together.* As a family, intentionally celebrate when one member accomplishes something significant.

7. *Set the example.* It's essential that you, as the parent, practice what you preach.

By becoming an encourager, you help to draw out the very best in your child. That's what Hunter's dad did on the day of their cold November hike. It's what Jack's dad didn't do.

Improving Your Positive-to-Negative Ratio

To this list of seven principles, we want to add five more practical suggestions from our own experience as parents and family educators. Psychologists say that it takes five positive statements to offset one negative statement spoken to a child. And that's just to stay even!

What can we do to make sure that in our own statements, our positive-to-negative ratio is at least five to one?

1. *Keep a list of your positive and negative comments over the next twenty-four hours.* You may be surprised to see how negative you really are, and you will be encouraged to focus more on the positive.

2. *Ask God to help you see the positive side of your child's temperament.* Read Philippians 4:8 (we talked about this verse in the last chapter) and practice reframing your child's negative extremes into positive qualities.

3. *Help your child identify natural abilities and interests.* A child who develops competence and confidence in at least one area will be better able to weather the feelings of inferiority that are almost inevitable in the preadolescent years.

4. *Find good outlets for your child's energy.* Spirited children are often bubbling over with energy. Can you think of a sport or activity that might be an appropriate outlet for some of that energy? One mom wrote us and said that her son had taken up karate. "We found that physical exercise helps our son calm down," she wrote. "Someone suggested to us that the martial arts are good for the volatile child because it is physical release in a controlled manner. For the spirited child, this is important."

5. *Make complimenting your child a habit.* Research says it takes three weeks to develop a new habit and six weeks to feel comfortable about it. For the next few weeks, practice giving your child a compliment each day. Be sincere!

According to Adele Faber and Elaine Mazlish, in their book *How to Talk So Kids Will Listen and Listen So Kids Will Talk*, helpful compliments come in two steps. First, we describe what we appreciate about our children. And second, after hearing our descriptions, our children are able to compliment themselves.[3] Here's an example of how it works:

> *Mom* (to son): "I really appreciate the way you kept the baby happy this afternoon. I was able to get my editing job done, and it was great to hear the two of you laughing and having fun."
>
> *Son* (to himself): "I'm a good baby-sitter. I really helped my mom."

Mistakes to Avoid

Some parents work hard to build their children up, only to tear them down again by making some common parenting mistakes. If your goal is to be a true encourager, here are a few things you will want to avoid:

- Calling your child "good" or "bad" because of something he or she did. Talk about the behavior instead.
- Using unkind nicknames such as "Shorty," "Chubby," or "Klutz."
- Comparing one son or daughter with another. Years ago we heard Dr. James Dobson, author of *The Strong-Willed Child*, say that comparison is the root of all agony. He's right!
- Criticizing your child when he or she makes a mistake.
- Not letting your child take risks.
- Withholding physical affection. All kids need hugs and kisses.

- Withholding responsibility. If your child is never given a chance to be responsible for something—say, taking care of a pet or completing a regular chore—he or she will grow up feeling insecure and incompetent.

Think of your child as a jigsaw puzzle that is only partially completed. Will you choose to see a beautifully developing picture in this precious life God has created, or will you concentrate on the missing pieces? With spirited children in particular, it's critical that parents hear their cry: "Please encourage me! Please see the positive in me!" If *you* don't hear your child, who will?

Taking Steps toward a Better Future

As a parent, you can take a number of practical steps to begin encouraging your child on a regular basis. In the last chapter, we listed Just-You-and-Me times and Family Appreciation Nights as tools for understanding your child better. These activities also present great opportunities for you to give your son or daughter much-needed encouragement. Here are a few additional things to try:

Make Birthdays and Holidays Special

Around the dinner table on birthdays or other holidays, ask each family member to state specifically what he or she appreciates about the one celebrating the special day. Serve the birthday person a favorite breakfast in bed. (That's what we did in our family.)

Pray before Bedtime

Pray with your son or daughter each night, and include a phrase or two thanking God for your child.

— Keep a Prayer Diary

This is an activity for you to do alone. In a notebook, make a list of general things you are praying for regarding your child and your relationship with him or her. On the next page, start a running diary of specific prayer requests. You don't have to write something every day, just when you feel the need—for example, when you think you're about to start nagging! Leave plenty of space to write in the answer to the prayer when it comes.

We have kept prayer diaries for many years. It's so rewarding to read back through them and see just how faithful God has been! We know this activity will encourage you, too, for many years to come.

— Take a Nature Hike

Go on a hike with your child and observe the wonders of nature. Talk about:

- the fact that God's colors don't clash;
- the way all of nature works in harmony;
- what kind of leaf your child would want to be and why;
- what color butterfly he or she would want to be and why;
- the uniqueness of each organism in nature—and each one of us.

Keep a Positive Log

On the first page of a small notebook, write a description of your child's unique personality. On the next page, begin a running diary of positive things you observe about your child. Date each entry. You don't have to write something in your notebook each day or even each week;

but whenever you observe something special or positive about your child, record it. Then, on those days you want to resign as resident parent, pull out your Positive Log and let it help you put things in perspective. Remind yourself that tomorrow will probably be better than today.

Create a Self-Esteem Passport

Using a small notebook or folded construction paper, make a "Self-Esteem Passport." Write down positive things you see in your child's life. Use these questions to help you get started:

- What makes your child an "original"?
- In what areas has your child shown growth recently? Academics? Relationships? Sports? Accepting responsibility?
- How has your child shown personal courage? (Think of Hunter's hike in the woods.)
- How has he or she demonstrated self-confidence?

Attach a photograph of your child. Then let your child decorate the passport with "original art."

Play "Why I'm Me"

On index cards or notebook paper, have family members write descriptions of themselves. Then talk together about which of the traits they've named are inherited and which are acquired.

Put Together a Family Puzzle

Try to find a large puzzle of diverse people or animals for your family to work on as a group. For example, our family once put together a puzzle of 501 cats. It was a difficult feat because the cats were so much alike; yet each one, we discovered, was unique and had unique puzzle pieces that fit only that particular cat. As you put your puzzle together, talk about:

- the uniqueness of each family member;
- the way you fit together as a family;
- the fact that each of you are puzzles still under construction; no one is complete;
- whether it's better to concentrate on the missing puzzle pieces or the developing picture.

Getting Started Today

Remember, when you look at your spirited child, you are not looking at the finished puzzle. But rest assured that God does have the big picture in mind; and day by day, year by year, those scattered pieces are coming together to create a precious and unique individual.

Can you see it? Ask God to open your eyes! Then ask him to give you the patience, wisdom, and self-control you need to nurture and encourage your child to become the completed masterpiece he has in mind. With God all things are possible—including the transformation of your child's negatives into wonderful positives that honor and serve the Lord.

CRY #3

"You're *not* Listening!"

What it really means:
"Listen to me; talk to me."

It's the day before the first day of school. Your twelve-year-old daughter is suddenly out of control—yelling, slamming doors, furious with you and everybody else. When you calmly inquire about the problem, this is what you hear: "I have nothing to wear to school tomorrow!"

Forget that just yesterday you survived a marathon shopping spree to buy school clothes with her. When you suggest that she choose one of her new outfits, she responds, "They're all dumb. They don't fit right. I hate them, and I'm not going to wear them!"

Suddenly all of your parental wisdom and maturity zips out the window, and you're on the verge of screaming back something we could not repeat in this book. It's not enough to realize that this kind of behavior is typical for a spirited preadolescent who is anxious about facing the transition of a new school year. When you're the parent, the challenge is to keep from being drawn into your child's whirlwind of emotions. But how can you show love and support without being engulfed by the raging storm? Is it really possible to listen and talk to a human volcano?

Believe it or not, your spirited child, through this kind of frustrating, over-the-top behavior, is crying out, "Please listen to me. Please talk to me!" In this chapter we want to share with you how you can respond to that cry—and live to tell the story.

Understanding the Challenge

"I always dread going grocery shopping with my daughter," Nancy, the mother of four-year-old Caroline, told a group of sympathetic friends. "Whatever she sees that catches her fancy, she wants to buy, and she throws a tantrum if I don't give in to her wishes. Yesterday she wanted to buy every sweet cereal on the shelf! Then she talked incessantly up and down the aisles. I had had enough by then, and since I was hurrying to get home before my son got home from school, I basically ignored her—I just gave her a grunt or nod here or there. Then, at the checkout counter, she shocked me when she said to another shopper in the line, 'Gee, I wish I had a mother who could hear me!'"

What about *your* child? Do you think he or she could have the same complaint about *you*? Think back over the past couple of days. Can you remember a time when you tuned out your child while he or she was talking to you? Perhaps you were hearing the words, but you really weren't listening to what your child was trying to say. The truth is, spirited children are often more talkative and opinionated than other kids. Sometimes it's difficult to listen to their continuous barrage of emphatic statements and strong opinions—and equally hard to know how to respond.

As we noted in the last chapter, our children develop their concept of themselves in large part from the way they think that we, their parents, see them. Children who sense that they are loved and respected by their parents are more inclined to recognize and believe in their own worth as individuals. So how do we show our kids that we love and respect them? One of the most significant ways is to listen—*really listen*—to what they are saying. Communication is our lifeline when it comes to maintaining a positive relationship with our spirited children. As authors Adele Faber and Elaine Mazlish are fond of saying, we just need to learn how to talk so our kids will listen and listen so our kids will talk.[1]

Dealing with the Present

Every human being needs to feel understood. Stop for a moment and think: Isn't it wonderful when someone really understands and cares about how you feel? We can handle pressure better if we know that there's at least one other person who understands what we're going through.

You can be that person for your child if you're willing to identify with his or her feelings and really *listen*—not simply react, lecture, or advise. Sometimes we just need to open our ears and our hearts and save the advice for the family dog! It's not enough to *hear* our children's words; we need to listen for the *meaning* of those words. We should never assume that we know what our children mean simply because we heard what they said.

Let's say, for example, that your six-year-old daughter screams, "I hate my brother!" If you simply *hear* that statement, you may be inclined to react and scream back, "How can you say such a thing? You shouldn't hate your brother!" But if you're *listening* to your daughter, you might respond with a statement that recognizes and validates her feelings—something like, "Sounds like you're feeling angry."

> *Sometimes we just need to open our ears and our hearts and save the advice for the family dog!*

Sometimes when our children talk to us, they just need to be heard. They need to have someone identify with their feelings (not necessarily agree with them). Spirited children, in particular, can be very sensitive;

they feel things deeply and get their feelings hurt more easily than children who are easygoing. For them, the tears that always seem to be near the surface aren't a put-on. And if they're defiant as well as sensitive, they are likely to express their hurt feelings with anger. Listening to them can be difficult—but it's imperative that we understand the real meaning of what they're trying to express. If we immediately jump in, criticize, and try to solve all their problems, we haven't really listened.

Learning to Listen for Emotions

A big part of listening is understanding the *emotion* behind what is being said. Of course, in and of themselves, emotions are neither right nor wrong. If a child feels sad, he or she feels sad. For a parent to say something like, "It's wrong to feel sad; think of all the things you should be thankful for!" only shuts the door on real communication. Instead, we need to allow our children to tell us how they feel. By letting them vent their strong or volatile feelings to us, we defuse any potential explosion—kind of like letting a little air out of a balloon before it pops.

We won't always understand our children's emotions, of course, but we need to have our antennae up. With difficult or spirited children, it's especially important to be tuned in to even slight changes in their emotions. That way we can head off trouble before their feelings overtake them and make them incapable of thinking through a situation rationally.

Being an Emotional Coach

John Gottman, in his book *Raising an Emotionally Intelligent Child*, gives excellent advice on how to listen for and interpret our children's emotions.[2] He encourages parents to think of themselves as "emotional coaches" trying to get their kids to open up and reveal their true feelings.

To be good coaches, Gottman suggests, we need to look for ways to empathize and validate the feelings our children express. Let's say your eleven-year-old son complains, "That biology test was totally unfair. The teacher asked questions on things we never covered in class. It's just not fair!" You might be tempted to shoot back, "Well, son, I guess you didn't study enough," or "Are you sure you studied the right assignment?" But those responses, most likely, would only fuel your child's fire and provoke an argument.

A more reflective, validating comment would be something like, "You must really be frustrated!" Such a statement keeps the communication lines open and allows you to help your son process his strong feelings. It also puts a damper on a potential firestorm. Even a strong-willed, spirited child is hard pressed to argue with someone who is empathizing with him!

Putting a Label on Feelings

Gottman also encourages parents to help their children label their emotions by putting language to them. When we do this, we show our kids that we're not dismissing their feelings; we're empathizing with them and taking them seriously.

One clever mom we know helped her spirited preschooler identify her emotions by making a "mood chart" and hanging it on the refrigerator door. With Velcro she attached different colors of felt to corresponding pictures of faces showing different moods. Gray indicated tired; blue meant disappointed; red, angry; black, sad; yellow, happy; green, OK. When her daughter was having a difficult time expressing

59

herself, she would ask, "Which color (or picture) best describes the way you are feeling?"

Putting words to emotions helps children—and parents—deal with even the most trying circumstances. Take five-year-old Brooke, who'd been playing for several hours at a friend's house. When her mother came to pick her up, she stomped her feet and cried, "No, I'm not going home! I'm staying here. You can't make me come with you!"

"Brooke," her mother replied, firmly taking her hand, "I understand how you feel. You don't want to go home right now. You're having fun with your friend, and you want to stay and play some more. But now you have to go home."

Brooke put up a fight, and Mom continued to identify with her feelings: "Honey, I know you're very disappointed that you can't play longer. You are angry that you have to go home. But it is time to go, and you will have to come with me." Remaining composed, she gripped Brooke's hand and firmly guided her into the car. Brooke eventually calmed down on the ride home. But even if she had cried the whole way, she would have known that her mother really did understand how she felt. She would also begin to get the idea that temper tantrums are an ineffective way to get Mom to give her what she wants.

Communicating How You Feel

Feelings are important, and children—especially spirited children—need to express them. That's not to say, however, that children should be allowed to be rude or hurtful for the sake of self-expression. As parents, it's our job to set limits for the appropriate expression of emotions. It's also our job to be models for our kids. That means that in addition to listening for our children's feelings, we need to express our own feelings in a way our kids can understand.

When our sons were growing up, we used a simple exercise to help us communicate emotions. First, we stated how we felt about a given situation, starting the sentence with the words "I feel..." Then, after expressing our emotions, we'd say, "Now tell me how you feel about this." For example, I (Claudia) might say, "I feel frustrated when dirty dishes are left in the living room. It's extra work for me, and it would be so simple for you to take them to the kitchen." Our spirited son would reply, "Dirty dishes in the living room don't bother me at all!" And while that wouldn't be the answer I was looking for, at least we could laugh together, and I'd know that he got the message: Mom doesn't like dirty dishes in the living room. We'd be able to talk about the mess without provoking an argument.

When we express our own feelings and then ask for a feelings response, we give our children the opportunity to express their emotions without feeling they've been attacked. And because they don't get defensive, we can deal much better with whatever issue is at hand. Sometimes they even surprise us by responding, "Gee, Mom, I'm sorry I left the mess in the living room. I'll try to remember to bring the dishes into the kitchen next time."

The Feelings' Formula

1. "Let me tell you how I feel. I feel..."
2. "Now tell me how you feel."

Interestingly, not only do we teach this exercise in our parenting seminars, we also teach it to husbands and wives in our marriage seminars. We've found that in almost any situation it helps people share how they feel so the other person can understand.

Getting Your Child to Talk

Sometimes it seems as if spirited children express their thoughts and emotions nonstop. Other times, when we really *want* them to tell us how they feel or what's going on in their lives, getting them to talk is like pulling teeth. So how can we make sure the lines of communication keep flowing both ways?

Listening is one sure way to get our children to talk. When we listen with interest, they feel that their ideas are valued, and their sense of self-esteem and confidence is built up. They reason, "If my parents believe I'm worth listening to, I must be a person of value and importance." When our children feel good about who they are, they are much more willing to open up and talk to Mom or Dad.

Here are a few additional keys to getting your child to talk—*really talk*—to you:

1. Be attentive when your child wants to talk with you.

Stop what you're doing as soon as you can and give full attention. Put down the paper or the dishes, turn off the television, and focus on your child. Remember the importance of eye contact, and let your non-verbal cues say, "I'm available to you." Be sensitive to your child's tone of voice and facial expression.

Really work at understanding what your child is trying to say to you by completing the "communication circle." In a communication circle, the first person makes a statement. The second person says, "What I hear you saying is…" and interprets what the first person said. The first person then affirms the interpretation or repeats the statement with greater clarity. The circle continues until both people have understood the same message. The goal of the communication circle is to understand what the other person is saying—not necessarily to agree or to put words in the person's mouth that he or she didn't really mean. Does this approach sound too difficult to do with your child? A few moments of this kind of focused attention can actually take less time and effort than the confusing, escalating battle of words that can result from a misunderstanding!

2. Encourage talk.

Smile, nod, and give short, one-word responses to indicate your interest. Keep questions brief, open, and friendly, and try to avoid asking "why" questions, which tend to make a child feel under attack. State your concerns in other ways.

When your child's standard responses are one-syllable grunts or words like "nope," "uh-huh," or "yep," try playing "communication tennis." With a tennis ball in hand, make a statement or ask a question that requires a response. At the same time pitch the tennis ball to your child. Your child responds to your statement or answers your question and then, as he or she pitches the ball back to you, makes a statement or asks a question that requires *you* to respond. See how long you can keep passing the ball back and forth. This is a good way to help children learn to initiate and carry on a conversation. If your child thinks games like "communication tennis" are silly and won't cooperate, try opening conversations with open-ended statements such as, "What I like best about myself is…" or "If I had three wishes, I'd wish for…."

3. Empathize with your child.

Try to put yourself into your son or daughter's shoes. This may take imagination and patience, but you will understand your child's actions and reactions much better if you try to identify with his or her feelings. Think back to your own childhood. Chances are you were a spirited child too! Try to remember some of your own strong feelings and how you dealt with them. Make comments such as, "You must feel proud of yourself for finishing that puzzle," or "Bet you're disappointed that your friend can't play with you this afternoon," or "You must be happy that your homework is done and you can get on the computer now."

4. Avoid "you" statements.

Often sentences that begin with "you" attack the other person: "You never pick up after yourself." "You are so inconsiderate." "I" statements are much safer. They express your feelings without leveling charges against your child. Remember the Feelings Formula? Start your conversation with "I feel..." and then ask your child to say how he or she feels in response.

Even worse than "you" statements are *absolute* "you" statements. "You never..." or "You always..." will get you in trouble every time!

5. Show respect.

Try to react to your child as you would to an adult friend. Listen as much as you talk. Face the fact that kids are complainers at times—especially if they're reactive or sensitive. Let your child get his or her grievances out in the open. Sometimes what your child needs most is simply to have you listen and understand.

6. Be flexible.

Being flexible and creative is necessary, especially when your child reaches the adolescent years. Look for opportune times to talk—for example, on the way to your child's dental appointment or on the way home after soccer practice or ballet. Drive time in the car can be a great communication time!

7. *Step back and pretend your child is someone else's.*

Yes, for the moment, pretend your son or daughter is your best friend's child! It will help you see your child in a whole new light. We often are more understanding with other people's children than we are with our own.

8. *Avoid knee-jerk reactions.*

It's so easy to respond to a spirited child in a knee-jerk sort of way. The problem is, those kinds of immediate reactions are almost always ineffective. The last thing you want to become is a drill sergeant, shouting out orders to your child that simply don't work! Take a look at the following situations, which show a typical knee-jerk reaction—and a better alternative response:

> **Situation:** Your child won't get out of bed in the morning.
> *Knee-jerk response:* "Get up, you lazy head! This is the last time I'm going to call you!"
> *Instead say:* "Good morning. It's 7 A.M. What should you be doing now?"

> **Situation:** Your child won't do his or her chores.
> *Knee-jerk response:* "When are you going to learn how to be more responsible?"
> *Instead say:* "We can't eat dinner until the table is set."

> **Situation:** Your child is fighting again with siblings.
> *Knee-jerk response:* "How many times do I have to tell you not to fight? You should love each other and be kind!"
> *Instead say:* "Do you need help or can the two of you work it out yourselves?"

9. Realize that every moment is not a great time to talk.

Regardless of how clever you are or what good communication skills you use, your child will clam up and be uncommunicative sometimes. An important part of communication is realizing that you may need to back off at times and give your child some space.

Other times your child will be talking (perhaps very loudly), and you will need to say, "Time out." You can't reason with a child who has gone "over the top" emotionally or who is clearly trying to manipulate the situation. You'll end up with a prolonged argument. At such times it's best to take a break and return to the issue later when everyone can deal with it more constructively.

10. Be willing to apologize when you are wrong.

If you don't know this by now, trust us: There will be times when your spirited child will almost drive you crazy. You will say things you'll regret. When this happens, be willing to apologize. In his book *The Dangers of Growing Up in a Christian Home*, psychologist Donald Sloat states:

> Although it is distressing, and even embarrassing, to admit that we don't have all the answers or that our behavior isn't always consistent with our stated beliefs, everyone can benefit if we handle it properly. Our children know the truth about us anyway, and instead of losing respect, we will gain more of their respect when we admit we're wrong and don't have everything figured out. Admitting your shortcomings helps your children see that life isn't always perfect and free from struggle. This gives them the freedom to be comfortable with their own struggles and feelings.[3]

Itsy-Bitsy Spider

We weren't perfect parents—just ask our three sons—and we assume you aren't either. It's OK to admit it. While we worked hard to communicate with our boys in positive ways, from time to time we would get into negative patterns and blow it, especially with our most spirited son, who would respond like a spider.

Have you ever watched what a spider does when you poke it? It either runs away quickly or draws its legs up into a little ball for protection. That was my son! (Of course, some particularly difficult spiders will try to take on their perceived enemy, no matter what the size difference.)

Does your child act like a spider when "poked"? Does your five-year-old pout? Does your teenager withdraw emotionally? Does he or she close up, even when your poke was unintentional—or when you didn't think it would have hurt?

Face it. As parents, we won't always be right. We won't always do things the best way. And sometimes our spirited children will become frustrated to the point of tears during conflicts with us—not so much because they think we are wrong, but because they feel we've handled the situation poorly. If that's the case, we need to apologize. We need to model the behavior we want our children to exhibit. And when we see our children retreating from us, we need to take the initiative to help them communicate their hurt feelings. We should always be willing to take the first step of apologizing or forgiving.

Ephesians 4:29–32 is a helpful passage of scripture for dealing with our children's strong emotional reactions. Paul writes:

> Do not let any unwholesome talk come out of your mouths, but only what is helpful for building others up according to their needs, that it may benefit those who listen. And do

not grieve the Holy Spirit of God, with whom you were sealed for the day of redemption. Get rid of all bitterness, rage and anger, brawling and slander, along with every form of malice. Be kind and compassionate to one another, forgiving each other, just as in Christ God forgave you.

Another good scripture is Proverbs 15:1, which tells us that "a gentle answer turns away wrath, but a harsh word stirs up anger." When we communicate with our spirited children, we should speak gently. (Yes, it's possible to be gentle and firm at the same time!) Our gentleness just might encourage our kids to open up and reveal their true feelings.

Volcano Revisited

Remember the human volcano at the beginning of the chapter who has nothing to wear on the first day of school? If she's *your* daughter, how can you apply the principles we've talked about in this chapter?

First, remember that you don't have to respond to everything your child says. And telling her, "Relax! This is no big deal," won't help at all. Instead, acknowledge her feelings and let her know that you're concerned about the problem, even though you won't be solving it for her. You could say, "I'd like nothing better than to come up with a fabulous, knock-'em-dead outfit for you to wear tomorrow, but you're going to have to figure this one out yourself." Then you could add, "I know this is really important to you, and I know you can deal with it."

What does your daughter hear? "Mom thinks I'm competent. She thinks I can handle it. I guess I *can* handle it."

Taking Steps toward a Better Future

To improve communication with your spirited child, you need to look for times to communicate! We already mentioned that time in the car, driving to appointments or practices or meetings is a good option. Time in the kitchen is great too. (Our boys were often lured into conversation by a plate of freshly baked cookies on the kitchen table.) Or why not take your son or daughter out to McDonald's for a hamburger and a milkshake, or plan some other Just-You-and-Me time? Think creatively, and you'll find those perfect opportunities to talk alone with your child.

Here are some other ideas to help you and your child communicate:

Write Notes

For years I (Claudia) included a note in each son's lunch box every school day. It was a way to give affirmation and let them know I was thinking about them.

Writing little notes can help you get over some bumpy patches. Here's a sampling:

- "Please hang me back up when you finish using me. Thank you, Your Towel."

- "I desperately need a walk! Your Dog."

- "These magic cookies, when eaten, will make you want to clean up your room!"

- "Caution: I am a human time bomb about to explode. Do not talk to me for ten minutes." (This note was pinned to the skirt of a particularly frustrated mom!)

Play "Name That Feeling"

Take turns identifying facial expressions. Make a face and let your child describe it as "an angry look" or "a happy look." Then let your child make a face, and you guess. You can also look through magazines together and identify the feelings of the people you see in the pictures.

Talk, Don't Bug

For the next twenty-four hours, try talking without bugging. What's the difference? According to one of our sons, talking is when you talk to your child but don't want anything—you have no hidden agenda. Bugging is when you talk in order to get your kid to do something. For an entire day, try to avoid bugging, manipulating (however subtle you think you are), or giving advice. It won't be easy!

Play "Tell Me About…"

Think back to when you were your son or daughter's age. Tell your child about an event or situation from your childhood that:

- was funny

- embarrassed you

- was hard for you

- made you feel proud

They may be amazed to find out that you made your mother angry, struggled with your temper, or had embarrassing moments.

Adopt a Family Puppet

If you have a young child, consider "adopting" a family puppet. Puppets are great for kids who are shy, stubborn, or just don't like to communicate. It is often easier for them to express themselves through a puppet than to tell you things face to face.

Choose from the large selection of cute puppets in your local toy store, or make your own puppet out of an old rubber glove, a sock, or a sack. To get conversations going between your child and this new puppet friend, have the puppet make open-ended statements for your child to fill in, such as:

- If I had three wishes, I'd wish for....
- The thing I like most about my family is....
- When I grow up, I'd like to....
- If I were a parent, I would....
- What I like best about myself is....

Adopt a Communication Rule of the Week

Emphasize good communication as a family by developing your own "Family Communication Rules." Write the rules on slips of paper and put them in a jar. On a designated day each week, draw out that week's rule. Here are several family-tested examples:

- Week One: *Don't make "you" statements—only "I" statements.* The first week we tried this communication rule, there were a lot of uncompleted sentences in our house. But there was also less negative communication. We found ourselves beginning to say things like, "I would appreciate it if you would take out the trash" instead of, "You never take out the trash!"

- Week Two: *Pay attention to each other's emotional changes.* If your child is young, you might want to adopt the emotional grid we talked about earlier and use felt colors to identify emotional states.

- Week Three: *Express your feelings, but be willing to listen to the other person.* This rule helped our family to get issues out in the open and attack them instead of each other.

- Week Four: *Say positive things*. Every day have each family member try to say at least one nice thing to each of the other members of the family.

Give "Good Listener" Awards

Each week, show how much you value good listening skills in your family by giving the person who has best modeled those skills an award—perhaps a medallion with this phrase from James 1:19 engraved on it: "Everyone should be quick to listen, slow to speak and slow to become angry." Or give the award to the person who is "most improved."

Have a Family Scripture Memory Challenge

Have every family member memorize Ephesians 4:29–32. Reward the first one to complete the memory work. Give another award when you observe the scripture being applied.

Getting Started Today

Good listening and communication skills do not come naturally or easily—for adults or children. Rather, they're developed over time. As we begin to attune our ears to our children's emotions and really *listen*, we put ourselves in a better position to identify their needs and help them deal with their feelings and personal struggles. We open up the channels for the kind of communication that solidifies and enriches our relationships. Spirited children need parents who hear their cry— "Listen to me!"—and who respond to that cry with compassion, gentleness, understanding, and love. You can be that parent, beginning today.

"I Want *to do it* My Way!"

What it really means:
"Teach me how to cooperate."

"I can beat you to the computer," eight-year-old Preston shouted to his six-year-old brother, Nate.

"No, you can't! It's my turn to get on!" responded Nate.

"Is not!" screamed Preston.

"Is too!" yelled Nate.

Nate scrambled and beat his brother into the high-backed chair at the computer desk in the family room, but Preston wasn't about to give up the battle. He screamed and pulled and punched at his little brother. When he saw that Nate wasn't going to budge, his emotional thermometer shot up so high that he had a total meltdown. He began kicking furniture around the house and yelling, "Mom, Nate's wrong! It's my turn to play on the computer!"

Preston's mother intercepted him before too much damage was done. Calmly, she assured him that he would get a fair turn and suggested using a timer to keep track of each boy's computer use. But Preston's thermometer was already registering "beyond reason," and no compromise would satisfy him.

"I want you to go up to your room to cool down," his mom said gently. "By the time you come back downstairs, it will be your turn to get on the computer."

Instead of heading for the stairs, Preston screamed and stomped through the kitchen into the laundry room. The door slammed, and his mother could hear him punching, hitting, and turning over laundry baskets and storage boxes. When the noise subsided, she opened the laundry room door to find Preston sitting on top of the dryer with his legs dangling over the side, pushing down hard with his feet on the open dryer door.

What was this patient mom's response? Here's what she told us:

I could tell Preston was stretching the dryer door out of alignment, and I tried to tell him that—more loudly at this point. He replied with his standard answer for times when he's blown his top: "I don't care!"

At that point I was about to lose it too. I got him to hop off of the dryer, and because I'm learning more about what helps him to calm down when he explodes, I used the next few minutes to distract him by showing him how the dryer door is supposed to fit into the dryer—and how it didn't fit now. This gave him time to calm down enough to stomp around without further destruction and wait for his turn on the computer.

While this is not my idea of brotherly cooperation, I consider this incident a small victory because Preston calmed down enough not to hit me or scream, "I hate you!" And eventually he and Nate did take turns on the computer.

Now, every time I put clothes in the dryer, I'm reminded of how hard it is to get my difficult child to cooperate. Actually, I have to jimmy the dryer door with a dusting pole against the wall to keep it tight enough to run every time I turn the dryer on.

As many parents of spirited, difficult children will attest, Preston's story is not so unusual. Sometimes cooperation in the home takes as much work and maintenance as that bowed dryer door in the laundry room. Strong-willed children tend to want things their way—and if they don't get their way, watch out!

Just ask Ellie's mom, who agreed to help out in her four-year-old daughter's preschool classroom. Thinking that it would be a great way to teach her daughter about sharing with others, Mom brought one of Ellie's books to school to use as an introduction to a lesson. But when she took out the book and showed it to the class, Ellie shouted, "That's my book. I want it back right now!"

"Ellie," her mother said calmly, "you need to share your book with the class."

Ellie said nothing in response. She simply ran up to the front of the room and bit her surprised mother on the arm so hard that it made her scream!

Spirited children like Preston and Ellie have difficulty adjusting their desires to the needs or wants of others. They love challenges and hate ultimatums. The word *cooperation* isn't in their vocabulary; instead, their favorite phrase is, "I want to do it my way!" This independent attitude often appears early in life—as it did for six-month-old Lucy, who insisted on feeding herself. That spoon belonged to her and her alone, and woe to her mother if she tried to take it away!

Other children wait to demonstrate their "let me do it my way" independence when parents introduce the tug of war better known as "potty training." From the start there's no question about who's in control— and it's not Mom and Dad. Every parent who has gone through the potty battle knows, however, that it's only a minor skirmish in the larger parenting war. Cooperation is not something that's easily won. But you and your spirited child can *both* come out winners if you take the time to understand the challenge that's ahead.

Understanding the Challenge

Because of their inflexible nature, spirited, difficult children often lack the cooperation skills of negotiation and compromise that come easily to more compliant children. They tend to have an all-or-nothing mind-set and perceive compromise as "giving in." The rules and requests that are no big deal for easy-going children are like gasoline on a flame for more spirited types. Some children become so focused on a particular idea, goal, or desire—like Preston and the computer or Ellie and her book—that they seem to lose the rational ability to move on to an alternative plan.

As their parents, we need to understand that our spirited children are prewired differently than more compliant kids. They're not trying to drive us crazy—they just have a different perspective on life and a great need to blaze their own trail. Our job is to do all that we can, with God's help, to nurture and develop them into young people who consider the needs of others and handle disappointment and blocked goals with maturity.

Developing a Team Spirit

Ultimately, the determining factor in our children's willingness to listen and cooperate with us and with others is the relationship we develop with them. Studies show that child compliance rates vary based on how well parents connect with their children and how consistently they apply discipline.[1] We know from experience, however, that it's hard to connect with your child—even to *want* to connect—

when he or she is throwing one tantrum after another. And we know how hard it is to be consistent with discipline when you're being worn down and worn out day after day by your child's refusal to cooperate with even the simplest of requests.

Is it any wonder that difficult or uncooperative kids sometimes get the idea that we think they're the enemy? The truth is, spirited children have an intense need to know that, in fact, Mom and Dad are on their team—that we love them, accept them, and believe in them. They need to know that we're 100 percent behind them as unique and special individuals, even if we're not always 100 percent behind their behavior.

Anticipating Your Child's Frustration

Four-year-old Kayla never did well in stores. One afternoon, in typical fashion, she cried out for a candy bar on a nearby rack while her mother was in the check-out aisle paying for groceries.

"I want candy!" Kayla cried from her seat in the cart.

"No, Kayla, not today," her mother responded—at which point Kayla grabbed Mom's hand and dug her nails in so deep that she drew blood. Refusing to give in, her mother left the store with her hand bleeding and her daughter screaming.

Of course, Kayla's mom was well within reason to deny her daughter's request. Parents shouldn't give in to their children's every demand just to show they're "on their team"! But a wise senior team member will try to *anticipate the frustrations* of the spirited junior member—and avoid fighting unnecessary battles.

Ross Greene, in his book *The Explosive Child: A New Approach for Understanding and Parenting Easily Frustrated and "Chronically Inflexible"*

Children, identifies five characteristics of parents who've learned what it takes to develop team spirit.[2] Let's take a look at each one and see how they apply in Kayla's case:

1. *Parents have team spirit when they have a clear understanding of their children's unique difficulties.* Parents need to be aware of the specific factors that fuel their children's inflexibility or explosiveness. Kayla's mom realized that her daughter's behavior, while not acceptable, was somewhat predictable.

2. *Parents have team spirit when they try to identify—in advance—specific situations that routinely lead to trouble for their kids.* Many parents find it helpful to keep an informal diary of their children's meltdowns over several weeks so they can begin to recognize patterns and anticipate difficult behavior in the future. Kayla's mom knew beforehand that her daughter had a hard time on shopping trips. She could have headed off Kayla's demand at the pass by either forewarning her daughter that she wasn't going to get a treat on this trip or by taking the initiative to get her a lollipop or a box of Animal Crackers early on.

   One mother we know set up a point system of rewards and told her spirited child, "When we go to the grocery store, we are only getting what is on my list. You may help me choose the jelly and the Pop Tarts. But please do not ask for anything extra. If you do, you will lose a point. If you cooperate, when we get home you will gain a point." By using this same technique before going to church, the mall, or other potential trouble spots, she avoided a great deal of embarrassment and struggle. Her advice to other parents: "Clearly state the rules before going in—even if you stated them last week!"

3. *Parents have team spirit when they read their children's warning signals and take quick action whenever these signals are present.* What warning signs did Kayla's mother miss? Before they arrived at the store, Kayla had fallen asleep in her car seat, and she had fussed when her mother woke her up and lifted her into the shopping cart. She was tired and cranky before the shopping even started—but her mother was too determined to get her shopping done to notice.

4. *Parents have team spirit when they understand how they may be fueling their children's inflexibility and explosiveness.* Kayla's mom realized in hindsight that she had put her daughter in a "meltdown" position by planning the shopping trip so close to naptime. She had also fueled the fire by ignoring several of Kayla's quieter attempts to get her attention as she hurried up and down the aisles.

5. *Parents have team spirit when they take into consideration both their own desires and their children's abilities.* Sometimes parents set their children up for failure by expecting a maturity and flexibility they don't yet have. If Kayla's mother had weighed the importance of her shopping trip against what she knew about Kayla's temperament, she might have chosen a different course that would have worked better for "the team." For example, she could have timed the shopping trip for the morning, when Kayla was typically bright and happy. Or she could have hired a sitter to watch Kayla (or waited for her husband to come home) so she could go to the store alone.

For the most part, Kayla's mom didn't show much team spirit that day in the store, and her daughter's meltdown was the result. What about you? Do you have team spirit when it comes to your relationship with your spirited child? Which of the five characteristics do you need to work on?

Dealing with the Present

We're certain—whatever your child's age—you've already learned that getting him or her to cooperate with you is one of the most difficult, frustrating, and time-consuming (not to mention emotion-consuming) tasks of parenting. As Dr. T. Berry Brazelton notes in his book, *Touchpoints: The Essential Reference*, provocative behavior is natural to kids; it's the way they test themselves and their limits.[3] But sometimes it seems as if parents are the ones being tested! Fortunately, Brazelton offers a number of tips on how to encourage kids to cooperate. For parents of spirited children, these tips are more than suggestions; they are lifesavers:[4]

- Before problems arise, discuss the issues you know might cause trouble. Openly present the choices involved and the way you'd like your son or daughter to behave. Have these discussions when your child is calm and under control— not when he or she is in the midst of a struggle.

- Respect your child's capacity to make the choices you offer. Gear the options to your child's age and his or her ability to maintain self-control, remember, and follow through.

- Examine your own tolerance for your child's misbehavior and determine if certain activities make you overreact.

- Join your child in doing what you want him or her to do. You'll not only provide a model, you'll foster a sense of communication between the two of you.

- Understand that the more you increase the pressure on your child to do a particular thing, the more his or her defiance will increase. Try to offer your child alternatives that have a similar goal.

- When you definitely want your child to do something, never ask, "Will you?" Instead say, "Now it's time."

- Praise your child whenever he or she achieves cooperation!

Following these suggestions will help you maintain open, honest communication with your son or daughter and avoid the manipulation and power struggles that sometimes go on when parents want their children to do something and the children don't want to do it. With your guidance, your child can *choose* to cooperate with you and feel the reward of achievement when he or she does.

Picking Your Battles Carefully

Of course, you can do all the right things and still struggle to get cooperation most days. Sometimes parenting can seem like a series of battles in a very long war! The good news is, not every battle needs to be fought. Let's face it: You're not going to win every fight. And you only have so much emotional energy anyway. That's why you need to pick your battles carefully—very, very carefully. Why get into a conflict with your son or daughter and destroy any potential for cooperation over a matter that is simply not that important?

Take a moment to think about your relationship with your child. What are the major issues you battle over? What are the minor ones?

Do you think your son or daughter would give the same answers?

Over the years in our seminars and PEP Groups, we've used two key questions to help parents determine whether a matter is major or minor—and whether or not it's worth a fight:

1. Is it a moral issue? (If the answer is yes, it's always major.)
2. What difference will it make in light of eternity?

These two questions can be invaluable, especially as children head into adolescence and the teen years. Things like hairstyles, clothes choices, and music volume are minor compared to more serious issues like drug and alcohol use, peer pressure, and faith in God. As we heard one youth pastor put it, "If it can be taken off, washed out, or cut off, don't worry about it." You don't want to use up all of your emotional energy fighting over minor issues; when a major issue comes up, you won't have enough left in reserve to take a strong stand. Asking, "Is it a moral issue?" and "What difference will it make in light of eternity?" can help you keep things in perspective.

In her book *You Can't Make Me—But I Can Be Persuaded,* Cynthia Ulrich Tobias suggests another important consideration in choosing which battles to fight: your child's physical safety.[5] What does a mother do when she gets in the car with her two-year-old son? She puts him in the car seat and buckles him in, of course! It's automatic. He may be screaming at the top of his lungs, but in the end Mom must win this battle every time. One of our grandsons is a very strong-willed little boy, but he's learned from experience that the seat-belt rule is written in stone. It's amazing to see how cooperative he is when he gets in the car these days!

One mother tells the story of her spirited preschooler, Matt, who continually tried to open the front door. They lived on a busy street, and it would have been very dangerous for Matt to venture outside alone.

Time after time Matt went to the door and reached for the knob, and time after time his mother said, "No" and physically removed him from the doorway. This went on for weeks, but Mom stayed consistent. Finally, Matt lost interest in the door when he realized his attempts to open it were futile.

When it's a matter of your child's safety, the issue is always major. It's a battle you must take up—and cannot lose.

Raising Cain and Abel

When our boys were growing up, a major issue in our family was sibling rivalry. And in fact, any parent with two or more children must deal to some degree with this challenge. But the problem tends to be magnified in blended families, families with adoptive children, and families with one or more difficult or spirited kids.

By definition, "rivals" are two or more people competing for the same object or goal, often displaying signs of jealousy and antagonism toward one another in the process. Siblings can become rivals:

- as they try to develop individual identities;

- as they pass through conflicting stages of development;

- when they experience unfair treatment or favoritism, whether real or perceived;

- when they get disappointed or frustrated by a parent for whatever reason;

- if they think they must compete for their parents' love and attention.

Because spirited children require more attention than compliant ones, it's easy for an easy-going kid to think a more difficult, time-consuming sibling is the parental favorite. It's just as easy for a spirited child to think the more compliant brother or sister—the one who never gets in trouble with Mom and Dad—is the favored sibling. And the truth is, parents may prefer one child's *behavior* over another, but families that have the most trouble with sibling rivalry are those in which the parents have difficulty distinguishing between *who* their children are and *how* their children behave.

Sibling rivalry is nothing new, of course. It existed between the earliest of siblings—Cain and Abel, Isaac and Ishmael, and Jacob and Esau, for example—and it continues today in families all over the world. But while it may be universal, it doesn't have to lead to murder, abandonment, or deceit, as it did for the three pairs of brothers in Genesis! You *can* minimize the impact of sibling rivalry in your family. Here are some steps to take to encourage good relationships between your children:

- *Avoid comparing one child with another.* We mentioned this statement by James Dobson in an earlier chapter: Comparison is the root of all agony. It discourages the less favored child and puts a terrible burden on the favored one. Don't do it!

- *Be fair with your children—and that doesn't mean be equal.* "It's not fair!" is one of the most common cries heard in any household with two or more children. Dr. Peter Goldenthal, a family psychologist and author of *Beyond Sibling Rivalry*, states that the more tuned in you are to the balance of fairness in your children's lives, the more you can do to reduce or even prevent sibling anger and family conflict.[6]

  The question is, what is fair? Since all children are different from birth, fairness should not be interpreted as treating all brothers and sisters the same, but rather treating them differently based on their unique needs. Treating your children the same at all times and in all situations is impossible— and trying it only encourages them to keep score and collect endless ammunition for petty arguments.

Growing up, our three sons were totally different. For example, one son was extremely responsible with money, while another had a difficult time managing whatever money he had. Considering these differences, we gave the more financially responsible son more latitude in handling his own money; we monitored the other son more closely until he showed that he could handle his finances. We loved them both, but treating them equally in this case would have been a financial disaster!

- *Respect the ways in which your children are different.* Help your children learn to respect their siblings by showing *your* understanding and appreciation for each child's unique qualities. For example, is one of your kids an extrovert and the other an introvert? The introvert may be very social, but he or she has a need for space and "down time." The extrovert, meanwhile, is energized by people and bored when he or she is forced to be alone or quiet. You can balance their conflicting needs by—remember our last point?—treating each child differently. You might arrange for the extrovert to participate in play groups or get together with friends, for example. Meanwhile, you'll want to think of quiet, more relaxing activities for the introvert. As the parent, your job is to see that both children have their unique needs met.

This point is especially important if you happen to be like us—you have all girls or all boys. You need to be especially

85

careful to recognize differences and avoid forcing your children into the same mold. Instead, help each one develop his or her own interests. If the first child excels in soccer, expect the second to go in a different direction (unless he is naturally a more talented soccer player!) By recognizing the uniqueness in each of your children and encouraging them to follow their own bent, you'll increase their self-esteem and reduce the tendency toward sibling competitiveness.

- *Resist the urge to be the referee.* Unless you are actually present and observe the cause of a conflict between two siblings, you probably will never know the "real" story. Most of the time your best course is to let them work out their disagreements themselves.

  One parent told us about an approach that works well for her. "We ask each son to tell his side of the story in the presence of the other. Each must be quiet while the other is talking, because we want them to learn there are two sides to every story. We usually do not referee unless someone is bleeding or something is broken. Often just getting heard helps to de-escalate the tension."

- *Avoid labeling your children.* No one wants to be known as "the difficult child," "the stinker," or "the messy one." But your difficult child is not the only one who can be hurt by labels. It's a heavy burden to be "the good kid" too.

- *Don't ignore accusations of favoritism.* Even if you think there's no basis for the complaint, hear your children out. Sometimes they need help identifying what they're feeling and venting those feelings in appropriate ways.

- *If a situation gets too heated, call for a cooling-off period.* When emotions are running high, take a time out before discussing the problem. It's easier to resolve a conflict when everyone involved has calmed down and each person can be more objective.

- *Accept that some sibling rivalry is inevitable.* While there are many things you can do to foster good relationships between siblings, the reality is that kids are kids, and life has its ups and downs. If you have more than one child, you *will* have squabbles and rivalry. But look at it this way: Conflict can actually help children realize that they are different from their brothers and sisters and that being different is OK. And the more they bump and rub together, the smoother and more refined they will become! As one parent put it, "Teaching kids to relate with siblings is the practice ring for getting along with others when they are adults."

  Ask God for wisdom as you guide the refining process, affirming each of your children as a unique and special creation. And on the days you feel you are losing the sibling war, remember: You are building for the future. This is only temporary. Your children will grow up!

An Apple for the Teacher?

Another big issue for our family was school. Like many spirited children, one of our sons was an uneven achiever. He would bring home A's and B's one grading period and C's and D's the next. If he didn't see a reason for completing an assignment, he didn't complete it. If a teacher was perceived as unfair, he figured, *Why should I care about this class?*

We discovered at parent-teacher conferences that our son's teachers either loved him or hated him—there was usually no in-between. For those teachers who saw him as bright, sharp, and even challenging, he excelled. But for those teachers who saw him as a problem child, he refused to cooperate and performed poorly, living up to their low expectations.

This was a difficult situation for us to deal with. It's one thing to work on cooperation in the home, where you have some semblance of control; it's quite another thing to get your child to cooperate when he or she is away at school.

A college professor and parent of a challenging child made this observation:

> Parents cannot control their children's grades. Ultimately the child decides what grades he or she wants. I see this all the time in college; the parents are frustrated because their son or daughter is not getting better grades. But the college student has control.
>
> Encouraging our children to do their best is important, but then we have to back off. It is my experience, as a parent and an educator, that we get the most frustrated over things we truly cannot control in our children's lives. We set boundaries for our children; we also need to set a few for ourselves and admit that some things are just out of our control.

The professor hit the nail on the head. Our children's academic issues are so frustrating to us because we can only influence—not control—the outcome. And since strong-willed or difficult kids tend to be underachievers or uneven achievers in school, those issues swirl frequently around them.

One year our son was convinced that a particular teacher had it out for him. We tried to help him understand that teachers aren't perfect—

they're human, and therefore they react differently to different children with different personalities. We explained that the way he related to this particular teacher affected the way she perceived him. What could he do to win her over? How could he do a better job of cooperating?

When things didn't get much better, we came up with a great idea: We would invite this teacher to our home for a meal. We would get to know her, she would get to know us, and she and our son would have a chance to relate to one another on a different level. But our strategy backfired. The next week our son lamented, "Things are even worse at school! Now my teacher treats me as her favorite!"

Sometimes, hard as you try, things just don't work out the way you planned. Still, we were on the right track. Seeking a teacher's cooperation in understanding and working with your spirited child often results in greater cooperation from your child in school. Check the article we've included in Appendix #3, "Surviving Parent-Teacher Conferences," for suggestions on communicating with a teacher on your child's behalf.

Making Mornings Manageable

Sometimes the hardest thing about school for parents is getting their children to cooperate in the mornings. Spirited kids, in particular, often don't handle time constraints well—making each morning a new challenge for Mom and Dad. This is no time to draw inflexible battle lines! Listen to one mom's story:

> When it comes to my son, Brent, I'm learning to be a little more flexible and to pick my battles. Our mornings have been going a lot better since we decided to let Brent eat what he wants for breakfast, as long as he is pleasant and doesn't pick a fight with his sister. Breakfast is no longer a

point of contention, and Brent still looks quite healthy. We just won't tell his pediatrician that he had a Diet Coke and Cheese Nips this morning! That's definitely not my kind of breakfast, but he did leave for school willingly, and the note his teacher sent home to us indicated that he ended up having a relatively good day!

Who says breakfast has to be eggs or pancakes or cereal and milk? If you're willing to be flexible and creative, mornings can be less stressful for both you and your child. Over the years, parents in our PEP Groups have shared a number of good ideas for managing morning madness. Consider trying one of these:

- *Let your young children sleep in their favorite sweat suits the night before.* Presto! The next morning they are already dressed and ready for school. (Of course, this doesn't work with clothes that tend to wrinkle!)

- *Prepackage your children's school clothes while you're doing the laundry.* As you fold the items, let your child put several school outfits together—complete with socks, underwear, ribbons, belts, jeans, and whatever else makes up a complete outfit. Then package each outfit or hang the outfits together in your child's closet. That week, instead of fussing about what to wear, your child can make a personal selection in record time. And best of all, everything will match!

- *Let your children take turns being the official "breakfast helper."* The breakfast helper sets the table the night before and puts out the milk, cereal boxes, butter, syrup, or other breakfast items in the morning.

Handling Times of Transition

Change is not easy for anyone. But when you put change, school, and spirited children together, look out! A transition time like the start of a new school year, for example, can be difficult for any child. But for spirited kids, who tend to feel emotions more intensely and often worry more, it can be even harder.

How does your son or daughter approach the first day of school? Some kids look forward to the start of school, if only to see their friends again after a long summer. Others, on that first day, bury their heads in their mothers' laps and soak them with tears, unwilling to budge. We remember how traumatic it was when our spirited son started first grade. Each morning he cried, complained of stomachaches, and offered at least a dozen other reasons why he should stay home from school that day. It took him until Christmas to get comfortable enough to go on to school without a struggle.

If your spirited child is having problems at school, ask yourself, "Has there been a big transition this year?" Changing from preschool to elementary school, elementary school to middle school, and middle school to high school are obvious transitions that can be scary for kids (and sometimes for parents too!). Here are some other potentially difficult scenarios:

- Your five-year-old has just begun going to school full days instead of half days.
- Your third grader has a strict teacher after several years of teachers with gentler personalities.
- Your fifth grader has been switched into an accelerated class and is concerned about keeping up.
- Your adolescent son is the only boy in his class who didn't grow six inches over the summer—or the only one who did.

- You moved, and your teenage daughter must start her junior year in a new high school with no friends.

Is this a year of transitions in your family? Take a "transition checkup" by making a list of recent transitions and changes that have occurred in your family and in your child's life. Did he or she just start wearing glasses? Discover a learning disability? Start a new after-school program? Begin a new sports activity? The changes can be big or little; remember, your spirited child is likely to have stronger feelings about a particular change than a more easy-going child.

So how do you help your son or daughter get through a transition? First, be ready and willing to listen. Be patient. "Don't trivialize their concerns with remarks like, 'Oh, you worry too much,'" suggests Lawrence Balter, psychology professor at New York University and author of the book *Who's in Control?* "Encourage them to talk to you about their fears."[7]

Look for ways to let your child know that you understand, that you're on his or her side. Plan Just-You-and-Me times. The effort you make to listen and spend one-on-one time with your child will not only show that you care; it will say, "You're not alone in this. We're a team. And cooperating together, we can get through anything."

Taking Steps toward a Better Future

As you begin to take steps toward a better, more cooperative future for you and your child, the following practical activities can help:

Have Morning Devotions

This is one routine that helped our family manage morning madness. The key, we found, was to keep the devotion times simple, relevant, and flexible. They rarely lasted over five minutes. Typically we chose a Bible verse each morning, read it out loud, briefly discussed it, and then prayed together. If one of our sons had a test that day, he was always willing to have us pray for him to do his best. But if one of the kids didn't want to participate in the prayer time, we didn't force him; we just remembered him in our own prayers.

A good way to choose a Bible verse each morning is to purchase a set of Bible memory cards or a "verse-a-day" flip calendar. Or you can make your own "Bible Verse Jar." Let each child write out several favorite verses on individual slips of paper, fold each one, and put the slips in a jar. Then take turns drawing a verse to read at breakfast.

Teach "One Body, Many Parts"

Together with your whole family, read 1 Corinthians 12:12–27. This passage emphasizes that Christ's church is made up of many different parts, each with its own unique strengths and weaknesses. Talk to your children about how they are different and how their differences complement one another. Discuss how each individual fits together with the rest of the family. This is a great way to keep your kids from falling into the comparison trap.

Beat the Homework Hassle

When it comes to homework, all children—and especially spirited, strong-willed children—need structure and discipline if they're going to succeed in school. Here are a few strategies to help foster cooperation:

- *Create a homework-helper box.* To remove any potential for the excuse, "I didn't do my homework because I couldn't find a pencil," or "I didn't have any paper," make a Homework Helper box. Purchase a cardboard storage box, and let your children decorate the outside of the box with stickers or stencils. Then stock the box with school supplies like paper, pencils, glue sticks, rulers, scissors, and a dictionary. Take your son or daughter with you to the store to select the supplies. Let your child make as many of the decisions as possible (for example, what brand or color to choose).

- *Designate a homework center.* If your kids are like most kids, they want to be near the hub of activity, and their bedrooms just don't qualify. One mom found a great solution: She created a homework center at the kitchen table. A file box held school supplies that were readily available—and that could be put away quickly when the table was needed for meals. (A Homework Helper box would fit the same bill!) With the homework center in the kitchen, Mom was always right there to answer questions and nudge her kids on to complete their work.

- *Start a homework notebook.* To keep an accurate record of homework—and avoid arguments about it—purchase a notebook and make entries in it for each of your child's homework assignments. (If you have two or more children, designate a section in the notebook for each child or use separate notebooks.) Also make note of each assignment's completion. Your child will feel a real sense of accomplishment as he or she is able to check off each task as "done."

- *Start the fifteen-minutes-a-day tradition.* Some children come home from school day after day with the same announcement: "I don't have any homework!" If that sounds like your child, start the fifteen-minutes-a-day tradition. If there's no homework to complete, encourage your child to do something educational for at least fifteen minutes to help develop the habit of studying. Even a spirited child will enjoy an occasional educational video, interesting computer program, or good book.

▬ Schedule Family-Together Times

Just-You-and-Me times can be very helpful when your child is struggling with cooperation. So can Family-Together times. In fact, having a regular time for the whole family to gather can help short-circuit sibling rivalries and other problems between family members. When our boys were growing up, we always made sure that our weekly Family-Together times were lots of fun. We played games, read, or did some other activity together. You might want to put together a puzzle, watch a home video, or go out for ice cream. The options are endless!

Getting Started Today

Teaching spirited children to cooperate is not something that can be accomplished overnight. Rather, it takes a sustained effort by creative parents who pick their battles carefully and look for ways to meet the unique needs of each individual child. If your son or daughter is struggling with cooperation, don't be discouraged. It *can* be learned. And according to God—who handpicked you to be your child's parent for life—you're the perfect teacher for the job.

CRY #5

"You *can't* Make Me!"

What it really means:
"Give me boundaries; discipline me."

"Mommy, I want that candy bar, and I want it right now!" three-year-old Ralph demanded, wiggling to stand up in the shopping cart.

"No, Ralph, I told you before we came into the store that we wouldn't buy candy today," his mother said calmly. "Now sit down in your seat."

"I want that candy bar, and I want it right now!" Ralph said again—much louder this time—as he tried again to stand up in the cart.

"No, Ralph. No candy today. Now sit down this instant! And please, use your inside voice."

Ralph's eyes narrowed and his face became flushed as he stood up in the cart like a three-foot-tall Genghis Kahn. "I want that candy bar, and I want it right now!" he shouted defiantly. Then he let loose a scream that resounded throughout the whole store.

His mother, of course, was completely embarrassed. She also felt utterly defeated. This was not the first time Ralph had refused to obey her in public, nor was it the first time he'd put on a full-fledged temper tantrum in a store. And unless something changed and changed fast, she knew it wouldn't be the last.

Temper tantrums are not unusual for children between the ages of two and four. But for spirited or difficult children, tantrums are almost a "signature" behavior, and they don't necessarily stop at age four. For some kids, the inability to handle frustration—manifested in an aggressive attitude that cries, "You can't make me!"—can continue for many years. (For some quick tips on diffusing a temper tantrum, see the box below.)

How to Tame a Temper Tantrum [1]

If your child is prone to temper tantrums, consider these tips from Dr. Lawrence Kutner, author of the book *Parent and Child*.

Relax. Take a deep breath. If your child is physically safe, waiting a few seconds to respond can work to your advantage.

Don't cave in. Remember that the absolute worst thing you can do is give your child what he or she is screaming for. It only reinforces the behavior for the future.

Take control of your child's environment. Remove the child from the site of the tantrum (even if it's only a few feet) to demonstrate that you are in control.

Explain why your child can't have what he or she wants, then stand your ground. Your immovability will speak louder than your words.

Don't be concerned about the people around you. Most parents have been in similar circumstances. They're probably empathizing with you, not criticizing you.

According to child psychiatrists, patterns of over-aggressiveness and difficult behavior may be rooted in a child's developing nervous system. Certain kids seem to be physiologically unable to control their impulses as much as other children their age. Because their nervous systems are less mature than other children's, they can't sit still for more than a few minutes. They are easily distracted. And once they begin to get excited or angry, they have difficulty stopping themselves. They are impulsive and have trouble concentrating on a task for more than a few minutes (or seconds, for some highly spirited types!) Dr. Lawrence Kutner notes that many of these children were restless before they even crawled or walked.[2] We know that our own spirited son fought with the car seat belt even before he was born. Whenever I buckled up, he would start kicking!

Did we just describe your child? Are you relieved to know that, most likely, your son or daughter came to you programmed that way, and it's not your fault? Your child's contrary, aggressive behavior isn't the result of something you have done wrong or failed to do!

And, just as importantly, it's not your *child's* fault either. At times, in the heat of the battle, it's easy for parents to attribute malicious motives to the angry little girl or guy who seems so bent on bucking them. But just as you shouldn't accept false guilt, don't affix false blame. And understand that despite all protests to the contrary, when our spirited children cry, "You can't make me!" they are really pleading for the clear boundaries and consistent discipline they desperately need to bring balance and order to their lives.

Understanding the Challenge

Next to love, discipline is a parent's second most important gift to a child, says child development authority T. Berry Brazelton.[3] And while most parents know that it's important to set boundaries for their kids, enforcing those limits in a consistent and effective way is one of the most difficult tasks of parenting—especially when a child is spirited.

A mother in one of our PEP Groups told us, "My five-year-old is very creative when it comes to boundaries. When I put him in time out, rather than sit in the chair, he will sit on the floor beside the chair.

When I ask him to leave his sister's doll alone, he will go and find another one of her dolls somewhere else in the house. When I ask him to sit in his seat at the table, he sits on his knees or squats in the chair. If I ask him to stop pounding the table, he taps quietly."

What's a parent to do? Strong-willed, spirited kids often stretch our concept of discipline (not to mention our patience) to the very edge. It's critical that we have a clear understanding of what discipline is—and what it is not.

We often equate discipline with punishment, but the two are not the same. The word *discipline* comes from the Latin word *discipulus,* which means "a learner." Essentially, discipline is about *teaching,* not punishment. As parents, our purpose in disciplining our kids is not to "give them what they deserve" but to teach them how to grow up and succeed in life—how to become mature, responsible adults who honor God and consider the needs and feelings of others. As Charlie Shedd says in his book *Letters to Philip,* discipline is "preparation for life at its best."[4]

The most effective forms of discipline take into account the ages, stages, and personalities of the children involved. There is no "one size fits all." And with spirited or difficult children in particular, discipline needs to be geared toward helping them develop self-discipline and self-control—two very important qualities necessary for their future success.

So what are the best ways to discipline a spirited child? What are the boundaries that need to be established, and how can they be enforced? Those are the million-dollar questions! When our spirited son was growing up, he knew how to push all the right buttons to make us go ballistic. If we went head-to-head in a verbal battle, he usually won. He easily could have grown up to be a rebellious young man. But we found the key to discipline for him: relationship.

Once, when he was about thirteen or fourteen, we told him how glad we were that he wasn't rebellious. He responded knowingly, "I have a tendency to be." Yet something had stopped him from becoming an all-out rebel. Intrigued, we asked him what advice he would give to a friend who was considering rebelling against his mom and dad.

"I'd tell him that he might get what he wants in the short term, but in the long term no one would win—neither him nor his parents," our suddenly-very-wise son said. "It's like standing on the edge of a cliff. You don't jump off because you know what the end result would be."

In that analogy our son was saying that he valued the relationship he had with us more than anything he might gain by rebelling against us! Apparently, over the course of his growing-up years, that relationship had become an ever-increasing motivation for him to curb his tendency toward rebellion and to learn self-control. And as you can imagine, when we heard this, we were motivated to work all the more to maintain a strong and healthy relationship with him.

If your child is spirited, aggressive, or rebellious, your relationship can make all the difference in the parenting years ahead. We believe that developing a strong relationship with your son or daughter is the first, most important step in setting and ultimately gaining your child's acceptance of appropriate limits and boundaries in life.

Dealing with the Present

How can parents establish boundaries, teach discipline, and build great relationships with their spirited children—all at the same time? Here are ten guidelines that can help.

1. Show respect.

As parents, we need to show respect for our children by listening to them, spending time with them, affirming their unique qualities, and encouraging them to develop their own talents and interests. And when it comes time to correct their behavior, we should continue to show respect. The discipline we teach should be for our children's good—not ours.

Think about the way God, our perfect heavenly Father, corrects us. His discipline is always in our best interest, as Hebrews 12:10 says: "God disciplines us for our good, that we may share in his holiness." God's discipline is designed to help us grow and develop and prepare for life at its best. The discipline we apply to our own children should have that same goal. We should respect them enough to discipline them with *their* best interest in mind.

That means we should never punish a child out of anger or frustration. A big emotional blow-up may feel good to us, but the child can be devastated in the process. It also means that we should attack the problem, not the person. There's a big difference between, "Lance, you're so clumsy! You spilled your milk again," and, "Oops! The milk is spilled. What's the best way to clean it up?" Or, "Danielle, why did you steal five dollars out of my pocketbook?" and, "We need to talk. I'm missing five dollars from my pocketbook. Do you know what happened to it?"

We show respect when we take the time to distinguish between defiant and childish behavior. For instance, did Lance spill his milk deliberately out of anger, or was it merely an accident? We also show respect when we get all the facts before convicting our kids. Is Danielle's mom *sure* that her daughter took the five dollars? And if so, does she know what motivated her to take the money?

2. Watch how you communicate authority.

Often the big problem for spirited children isn't *authority*; it's the way authority is *communicated*. "Just do it because I'm the parent and I

102

said so!" is almost always a precursor to rebellion and defiance. Our kids need to know the "why" behind our directives and have a clear understanding of what we think the problem is. Sometimes it helps if we ask if they see the situation as a problem too. As one parent put it, "If they disagree with your perspective, you can always say, 'I'm glad I asked if you saw this as a problem. Since you don't see things the same way I do, I would like to explain why I think we need to do something about this situation.'" If they understand our reasons, our kids are much more likely to comply with our requests.

Sometimes we can avoid our children's negative reactions by turning disagreements into constructive discussions. We can't always convince them that their opinion is wrong and ours is right, but we *can* provide them with a consistent model of constructive conversation, problem solving, and compromise. The communication skills we talked about earlier in the book can be helpful here—things like using "I" statements and avoiding "why" questions and "you" statements.

Take Chad's mother, for instance. She noticed that her spirited eight-year-old son, Chad, had gotten angry and had either hit or kicked his best friend, Taylor, the last few times the boys had played together. When she called Chad on his obnoxious behavior, however, he began making excuses and soon flew into an all-out protest. Realizing that her own frustration level was rising along with her volume, she decided she needed to refocus the argument.

"Chad, I understand you were upset with Taylor," she managed to say calmly, "but he was upset, too, with your hitting and kicking. There are better ways of handling anger than hitting. Friends don't like to be hit, and they won't remain friends when they're treated that way. Now is the time to learn some better ways to deal with frustration so that in the future you will have friends who like to be around you."

She knew that some of her words were going in one ear and out the other, but Chad seemed to calm down in response to her demeanor and approach, if not to everything she was saying. After that, the two were able to discuss the problem more rationally. By dealing with her frustration with her son in an appropriate way, Chad's mom gave him a model for handling his own frustration in the future.

3. Establish reasonable boundaries.

Boundaries give children a sense of security—they let them know what they can and can't do, where they can and can't go, and how they should or should not behave. Spirited children may try to push those boundaries; but the truth is, they need the security as much or more than their easy-going friends. Boundaries also help children learn to be responsible. Through the reasonable, age-appropriate limits and privileges parents set, they're encouraged to take increased responsibility for their own actions. (We'll talk more about developing responsibility in a later chapter.)

We set boundaries for our own sons when they were growing up. Each year, as they demonstrated an increased ability to make responsible decisions, we extended their "borders" a little more, giving them more freedom. Our goal was to raise boys who would be able to live responsibly on their own by the time they finished school and left home. For the most part, we succeeded!

One more point about boundaries: We can't expect our children to live within the boundaries we set for them if our own lives are spent pushing the envelope and bending the rules. Our children need to observe us living within reasonable boundaries too. We are models for our children, whether we choose to be or not!

4. *Clearly state what you want.*

Sometimes we get so good at telling our children what we *don't* want them to do that we forget to tell them what we *do* want! We shouldn't assume that our children automatically know what our expectations are in any given situation. And even if they do know, many spirited, strong-willed kids will be looking for the loophole. If you say, "Stop kicking the table leg," your child may start tapping on the floor, the chair leg, or the sibling sitting in the next seat. It would be better to state exactly what you want: "Keep your feet and legs still and quiet."

5. *Use positive reinforcement.*

Instead of always chiding them for bad behavior, we should compliment our children on their *good* behavior whenever possible—for example, when they remember to feed the cat, practice the piano without a reminder, or put away their toys. Pay particular attention to those things your son or daughter typically struggles with, and affirm your child when those issues or problems are handled correctly.

Positive reinforcement can be a very effective disciplinary tool, as we discovered when our sons were growing up. From time to time, we used charts and awards as incentives for good behavior. We adapted these incentives as the boys grew and matured. Stickers and treats may be great for young children, but elementary-age kids often prefer charting weekly goals. Older children can handle longer-range goals.

6. *Use "reality discipline."*

Whenever practical we tried to let our children experience the natural consequences of their actions. Dr. Kevin Leman and Randy Carlson, authors of *Parent Talk,* call this concept "reality discipline."

Using reality discipline, they say, keeps parents from having to punish their children and trains kids to be accountable and responsible. Instead of "playing the heavy," parents allow reality—and its consequences—to do the disciplining.[5]

For reality discipline to work, rules and agreements must be set up ahead of time with the understanding that if the child fails to obey the rules or meet the agreements, he or she will have to face certain consequences—many of which are natural consequences. Let's say, for instance, your teenage son is responsible for putting his clothes in the hamper when they need to be laundered, but they always end up on the bathroom floor. You may have to let him scramble around for clean clothes for a while until he gets into the habit of putting his dirty clothes in the proper place. Or say you have a fifth-grade daughter who calls home to ask you to bring her forgotten gym clothes to school—for the fourth time in two weeks. You may have to tell her to face the gym teacher without them this time. (You might also help her become more organized by adding a hook or shelf next to the front door to hold items needed for school the next day.)

7. Make the discipline fit the offense.

Withholding a privilege can be a useful form of reality discipline. The length of time that privilege is withheld, however, should fit the offense and the child's age. A four-year-old who colors on the wall, for example, may lose the use of the crayons for a few days; a thirteen-year-old who abuses his or her phone privileges may have calls restricted for a week. For the most part, the limitation of privileges should be reasonably brief; otherwise, kids can become overly discouraged. A month of no phone calls, for example, would seem like an eternity for a teenager—and probably for the rest of the household too!

8. Keep a "future focus."

When it comes to disciplining spirited children, our main focus should not be, "How should I punish my child for this offense?" but rather, "How can we avoid this situation in the future?" That's having a "future focus." We also demonstrate a "future focus" when we anticipate outbursts or challenges that may arise and plan in advance how we will deal with them. *Parent and Child* author Lawrence Kutner offers these suggestions for being prepared for the future:[6]

- *Look for patterns in what triggers your child's outbursts.* One mom says she has a four-point checklist: "Is he tired, hungry, lonely, or frustrated?" Try to recognize triggers and spot escalating behavior.

- *If you see a trigger, remove the child from that environment before he or she loses control.* For example, if your daughter is beginning to throw the Legos rather than build with them, remove the Legos and redirect her to another toy.

- *Provide structure.* Difficult or spirited children feel more secure when they have a predictable routine. By offering some kind of daily structure, you help your child remain calm and feel more in control.

- *Teach your child how to negotiate.* As soon as possible, teach your son or daughter appropriate ways to ask and negotiate for what they want. (We tell you how to negotiate a "contract" with your child later in this chapter.)

- *Focus on the positive.* The natural tendency for both children and parents is to focus on what's wrong with a situation rather than what's right. Look for the good in a situation and help your child see it too.

9. *Take a time out.*

"Time out" is not just a tool for preschoolers. All of us—parents and children alike—sometimes need a cooling-off period in order to get control of our emotions and regain a proper perspective so we can deal with a situation rationally.

What's the best way to do time out? Let's say your five-year-old son has just hit his little sister. Keeping your volume low and taking deep breaths to help you stay composed (the exercises learned in Lamaze class are wonderful for this!), calmly explain to your son that he must have a time out. Place him in a chair away from family activity, perhaps in another room; don't send him to his bedroom, where he would get distracted. Once he is sitting quietly and not trying to get up, set a timer for a predetermined amount of time. One minute for each year of age is a good guideline.

> *Our kids need to know: "Nothing you can ever do or say will be so terrible that I'll stop loving you."*

When the bell goes off, ask your son to tell you in his own words what he did that was wrong. Then encourage and assure him of your love and acceptance with a positive statement such as, "I love you, but you must not do that again," and give him a big hug.

Older children, too, can benefit from a period of isolation to think about what they did wrong and why their behavior was inappropriate.

If they're too upset to understand and acknowledge their wrongdoing, the time out can help them calm down enough to be able to discuss the situation more rationally. Of course, the exact procedure for the time out needs to be modified to take their age into account.

Then there are those times when a time out is necessary—and *we're* the ones who need it! One mother told us, "I once left my son wet and naked in his room while I put myself in time out. I needed a break! He wasn't toilet trained yet, but I figured if he wet the carpet, cleaning up the mess was better than hitting him—which I was tempted to do because I was at the end of my rope." Another mom said, "Sometimes when I put my three-year-old in time out—and if he continues screaming, and I'm close to the edge—I go out into the garage, get in the car, and just sit there so I can't hear him until the time is up."

Both of these mothers are very wise! They recognize their limits, and they know the value of a good time out.

10. Follow up.

As we mentioned earlier, discipline is all about learning. After imposing a time out or some other form of discipline, we need to follow up with our kids to be sure they have learned what they were supposed to learn. We also need to restore their sense of a loving relationship with us. Charlie Shedd calls this process "reattachment" and describes it as doing whatever we need to do to say "I love you." We may communicate our love by rocking our children, giving them a pat or a tickle, or going out for ice cream. However we "say" it, our love is basic to their sense of security. Our kids need to know: "Nothing you can ever do or say will be so terrible that I'll stop loving you."[7]

Taking Steps toward a Better Future

When it comes to teaching spirited children to respect boundaries and accept discipline, it's good to be proactive. Here are some ideas that can help:

Keep an "I Blew It" Diary

Many times in the heat of a battle, parents lose their cool and say things they later regret. To help break this cycle, keep a diary for several weeks. After a situation that gets out of control, write down what happened, how you were feeling before the incident, what triggered it, how you and your child reacted, and how you interpreted your child's behavior. After journaling a few times, you may begin to see a pattern. If your child is old enough, share your diary entries and talk about how both of you could have handled past incidents in a more appropriate way. Talk about how you would like to respond in the future.

Make a Family Calendar

Since difficult or spirited children tend to function better with structure, we suggest making a weekly and monthly family calendar. Include everyone's activities, from soccer practice and school programs to Family-Together nights and Just-You-and-Me times. Then sit down with your child and talk through the schedule. Having a calendar will ensure that a particular event doesn't catch your child unaware and throw a kink into the emotional works.

Reevaluate the Daily Schedule

In addition to making a family calendar, work with your child to come up with a reasonable daily schedule that includes times for getting up in the morning, going to bed at night, doing homework, playing, eating meals, and so on. Evaluate the routine on a weekly basis and adjust it as needed.

■ Institute a Family Council

Starting a Family Council can make your child feel valued, because it gives him or her the opportunity to have input into family decisions. It can also make planning and decisionmaking a lot more fun for the whole family. Listen to one parent's experience: "We started Family Council when our children were seven and three. Even at those young ages, the children enjoyed the council meetings, respected the decisions that came out of them, and learned how to lead meetings in a fun way."

Here are the rules for an effective Family Council:

- Anyone can call a Family Council meeting, but adequate notice must be given. No one can be forced to cancel previously made plans.

- All family members must be present to have a Family Council.

- The agenda is open. Each person has a chance to bring up anything he or she wants to talk about, whether action is needed at that time or not. No new topic can be brought up until the one being discussed is completed.

- The leader of the meeting rotates between family members. Minutes are kept to make sure there's no question later about who was in charge or what was decided. (A parent or older child should be the one to keep the minutes.)

- Parents have the right to say that a topic is open for discussion but not for a vote. (This comes in handy when children want to discuss chores and then vote not to have any.)

- Each person has one vote. The majority rules. A tie means no action—nothing changes. (Don't worry if the children outnumber the parents. Just be careful not to let things that would be hard on the family come to a vote.)

- Family members must vote based on what they think is best—not on how someone else wants them to vote. Each person should vote his or her heart. No deal making.

One family we know plans biweekly Family Councils. A fun activity is always included so that everyone looks forward to the meeting.

Negotiate a Contract

To establish appropriate boundaries with your child on issues that are negotiable, consider talking with your child about negotiating and working out a written contract. The contract should state explicitly what your child agrees to do and what you as the parent agree to do concerning a certain matter. Have both parties sign the contract, give a copy to your child, and keep one for yourself.

Simple contracts can be made as soon as your child can read and write. Even before your child has these skills, however, you can make a "picture" contract. (For example, you can use simple drawings to illustrate an agreement that says, "If you brush your teeth every night for a week, I will let you watch an extra video.")

How do you negotiate a contract with your child? Let's say your eight-year-old son wants to spend more time on the computer than you think is wise. You could negotiate a contract by following these four steps:

1. Have your son summarize what he wants: "I want to choose how much time I spend on the computer. I don't want Mom or Dad telling me when to get off."

2. Summarize what you want: "I don't want you to spend too much time on the computer and miss out on other good things like reading, playing with friends, doing chores, and spending time with the family."

3. Brainstorm possible solutions together. For example:

- Let the child monitor his own computer use and keep track of the time spent on it.

- Let the parent monitor the child's computer use and keep track of the time.

- Allow computer use only after chores and homework are completed.

- Have the child earn points toward computer use every time he does other constructive activities.

4. Work with your son to come up with a compromise, then write out your agreement in a contract. If your child happens to forget the agreement or tries to buck it deliberately, you can produce the contract and remind him of what you both promised to do. This will help you attack the issue and not your child!

An example of what a contract might look like can be found on page 114.

Getting Started Today

Setting and enforcing appropriate boundaries isn't easy when your child seems intent on bucking you and doing things his or her own way. But boundaries and discipline are exactly what every child—especially every spirited child—really needs.

So how do you begin? Don't try to put everything we've talked about into practice all at once. That would be an overwhelming task! Instead, choose one technique from this chapter and begin to work on it. Make one change at a time. By putting yourself on the right path today, you can give your child the boundaries and discipline that he or she is crying out for. It begins with one step.

Contract for Computer Use

The Agreement:

- During the week Billy agrees to complete schoolwork before getting on the computer.
- Mom will monitor schoolwork. Billy will show Mom completed schoolwork before getting on the computer.
- Billy can spend thirty minutes at a time on the computer, up to one hour a day.
- Billy will get off the computer whenever Mom or Dad needs it for their own use.

Consequences of Broken Agreement:

- First offense: No computer use for twenty-four hours.
- Second offense: No computer use for forty-eight hours.
- Third offense or beyond: No computer use for a period of time to be determined by Mom.

CRY #6

"I hate You!"

What it really means:
"Help me deal with my anger and frustration."

During one particularly long, cold winter when we were living in Germany, friends offered us the use of their chalet in Aldelboden, Switzerland. Just thinking about a weekend away in the Swiss Alps filled us with warm thoughts. It sounded relaxing—even though we'd have our three boys, ages three, six, and eight, with us.

We packed the car with food and gear and headed toward the Swiss border. Thankfully, the trip produced no major disasters—just the normal, "It's my turn to sit by the window." "No it's not! You sat there last time." "I'm starving." "I'm thirsty." "How much longer till we get there?" (Our standard answer: "Not over five hours.")

The next morning in Switzerland began early. After breakfast in the chalet, we set out for our major activity of the day: a long mountain hike. We were all excited. Everyone was cooperating!

Imagine majestic, snow-covered mountains on both sides of a narrow valley. A path winding through the towering trees. The first signs of spring peeping up through the melting snow. No televisions or stereos blaring. No cars or trains rushing by. Just wonderful silence—broken frequently, of course, by three very vocal young

115

boys who were actually getting along with each other. It was one of those Kodak moments.

Then we heard a noise—a rumbling noise that sounded like thunder. But it wasn't thunder. It was an avalanche!

Fear gripped our hearts. We had heard many stories about avalanches in the Alps, but this was our first encounter with one. We immediately swung into action. Picking up the three-year-old and encouraging the two others, we began to climb up as fast as we could to higher ground. Of course, if the avalanche happened to come down our side of the mountain, we'd be buried in snow—just a little higher up. But we figured we had to do *something*. When we saw tons of snow rolling down the mountainside across the valley, we all let out a big sigh of relief.

Parenting a spirited child can be a lot like that avalanche experience. Everything seems to be going along quite smoothly, then suddenly he or she explodes and dumps on you—not snow, but uncontrolled anger! Maybe your child stomps, hits, or throws things. Maybe he or she screams angry words, including the ones that always stab a loving parent in the heart: "I hate you!" The truth is, these words and actions reflect the heat of the moment; they're not the real message. What your child is really saying—pleading—is this: "Help me deal with my anger and frustration."

Understanding the Challenge

We can learn a lot about dealing with anger from the Swiss scientists who study avalanches. During avalanche season, these scientists anticipate potential disasters and set off little explosions along the mountainsides to keep snow from building up to dangerous levels. As parents of spirited kids, our job is a lot like that. We're called to anticipate our children's emotional avalanches and help them diffuse their anger in a way that keeps their frustration (and ours!) from building up to uncontrollable levels.

The trouble is, spirited children are wound tighter than more compliant kids, and they can be set off by the smallest thing. They go ballistic when we least expect it. And once their avalanche starts rolling, it's almost impossible to turn it back.

Look Out Below!

Anger is a scary emotion, especially when it comes from a spirited child. And because of its intensity, it is easily mishandled by the unsuspecting parents who are hit by it. The bad news is, when we don't deal with our children's anger in a positive way, we can create fear, anxiety, and despair in our kids—and sometimes in us.

After all, we're not exempt from angry feelings. Sometimes when our kids explode, we explode. Think back to the last time your child got really angry. How did you feel? Were you angry too? It's so easy to react to your child—and before you know it, you're both angry!

While raising our boys, we got angry sometimes. Once I (Claudia) told my kids, "I'm so upset right now. Please don't talk to me for at least an hour!" Another time, when I was on the verge of losing it, I said, "Stop! Hold everything. I'm upset, and I'm overreacting. But somewhere between my overreaction and no reaction is the right reaction, and if you give me a couple of minutes, I'll try to find it!" (Humor often diffuses a tense situation. I'll never forget the time one of our sons, in the middle of a very difficult discussion, looked up to heaven and said, "Humor, where are you when I need you?")

Ultimately, as parents, we must learn how to diffuse and process our own anger. Only then can we begin to help our spirited kids process theirs.

Be Angry, but Do Not Sin

Anger is not wrong in and of itself. In fact, according to the Bible, it's a God-given emotion. Ephesians 4:26 tells us, "In your anger do not sin." In other words, anger isn't sinful—but the way we handle it *can* be. Remembering this helped our family through a number of explosive episodes.

It also helped us to know that anger is a secondary emotion. It's usually the result of frustration or fear—both of which are common in families with spirited children. Take three-year-old Shane, for instance. Every afternoon while his mother runs errands, his teenage neighbor, Beth, comes to sit with him. And every afternoon, when Shane wakes up from his nap and sees Beth there instead of his mom, he screams, kicks, and runs from her.

Why is Shane so angry with Beth? She hasn't done anything wrong. But Shane's parents are going through a divorce, and his dad is hardly around anymore. Now it seems that Mom isn't there when he wants her to be, either. So he takes out his frustration and fear on Beth. Mom doesn't need to find a new baby-sitter; she needs to recognize that in this turbulent time in Shane's life, he needs extra assurance to know that he's loved and secure.

If your son or daughter is struggling with anger, think about the past several weeks and months. How often does he or she act out? What happens in those outbursts? What behaviors do you see over and over? Does your child get angry when he or she is tired, hungry, stressed? When things aren't going well at school? Is there something in particular that's frustrating your child?

118

Consider the family schedule. Is your child booked every day of the week? How many out-of-school activities does he or she participate in? One boy told us he hates Tuesdays because he has soccer practice and a piano lesson after school, and when he finally gets home at 7:00 P.M., he still has homework to do. That's a lot for anyone to be saddled with. No wonder this little guy is frustrated!

When frustrations or fears build up, anger is often the result. Fortunately our God, who is himself slow to anger and abounding in love, makes a way for us to handle our anger without sinning. Ephesians 4:26 continues, "Do not let the sun go down while you are still angry." Overcoming anger *must* be possible, because God never asks us to do something he doesn't equip us to do first. We may feel angry, but we don't have to blow up and hurt ourselves and others.

Our spirited children, who tend to be angry and frustrated often, can learn how to better manage their anger too. We can teach them appropriate ways to short-circuit blowups or handle them if they occur. That's our job as parents.

Here's one mother's story:

> Our daughter's thermometer fires up quickly. By the time we realize she's angry, she has already "lost it" emotionally. She has gone beyond reason and is incapable of making good decisions. With our other kids, we can calmly announce that a discipline will follow if they don't change their ways, and they accept that. But our spirited child takes it as a challenge. If we try to impose boundaries or discipline in the heat of the moment, she responds, "I *like* that discipline," or "I don't care," or "You can't do that. I just won't listen!"

We have found that if we let our daughter calm down in another room, have her go outside to take a walk, or remove her from the situation in some other way, she will usually get back to a point of reason. Sometimes we give her an hour or two of supervised "cool down" time; then we discuss what went wrong and what fair consequences would be. When we do this, she usually acknowledges what she did wrong and accepts an appropriate discipline.

This approach takes time and a lot of work. Sometimes we have to explain to her siblings that we are not just "letting her go." But this is the best way we've found to get through to her.

Because of her parents' efforts, this young woman is learning how to experience the valid emotion of anger—without sinning. She's learning to use self-control and process her strong emotions in a positive way. It's a lesson we all need to learn.

Dealing with the Present

The venting of emotions is necessary and even healthy in a relationship—especially a relationship between a parent and a spirited child. The question is, how will those emotions be vented? The answer is largely up to the parent. As we've said before, children learn to exhibit the behavior that's modeled for them. That's why it's so important for parents to learn how to process their own anger. Then they can teach their kids how to deal with anger not only through words, but by their example.

Identifying Anger

One concept that has been used successfully by many parents in our PEP Groups is the "anger ladder" developed by Dr. Ross Campbell in his book *How to Really Love Your Children*.[1] Picture a ladder with six rungs. The first rung is the worst way to handle anger; the sixth rung is the most appropriate way. The goal is to move up the ladder to a higher rung by learning to deal with anger in more effective ways. To illustrate how this works, consider the following scenario:

> It's a rainy afternoon, and Wesley and his sister, Sarah, are working on Sarah's new five-hundred-piece jigsaw puzzle. Wesley has just spent the last ten minutes examining every loose piece on the table, searching for a distinctly shaped section of sky, when Sarah smugly produces the piece. "Here it is!" she says triumphantly as she lays it in place.
>
> "Hey, where did you find that?" Wesley asks suspiciously.
>
> "I found it a couple of minutes ago and put it in my pocket," Sarah answers.

Wesley is angry! But what rung of the anger ladder will he react from? The answer depends on how well he has learned to handle his own anger. Here are the possibilities:

Rung 1: Passive-aggressive behavior

(Won't talk, but gets even.)

Wes might pretend to be pleased that Sarah found the piece and then secretly pocket a few pieces of his own. If Mom washes his pants later without checking the pockets—too bad!

Rung 2: Out-of-control behavior

(Hits people and breaks things.)

Wes might scream and yell, turn the table over, and destroy all the work that's been done on the puzzle, perhaps losing a few pieces in the process.

Rung 3: Fit of rage

(Hurts people by yelling.)

Wes might call Sarah a "cheater" and a "stinker" and tell her, "Do your own dumb puzzle by your own dumb self."

Rung 4: Uncontrolled verbal ventilation

(Yells and screams.)

Wes might yell but not be as destructive or mean as he would have on Rung 3. He might leave the room and shout, "I'm telling Mom!"

Rung 5: Unpleasant ventilation at object of anger

(Speaks harshly about the situation.)

Again, Wes might talk angrily, but he would be able to focus his displeasure: "You make me so angry! You hid the very piece I was looking for just to make me mad!"

Rung 6: Pleasant and rational ventilation toward cause of anger

(Expresses feelings appropriately—"I'm feeling angry because...")

At this level, anger is spoken with greater self-control than at Rung 5. Wes might say, "I'm angry because you hid the very puzzle piece I've been looking for. I don't enjoy playing with you when you tease me like that!"

If your child typically reacts at Rung 5 or 6, feel free to faint! If not, don't be discouraged. The object here is to help your son or daughter move up the ladder and learn to handle anger in more appropriate ways. If your child moves from Rung 3 to Rung 4, that's progress!

Learning to Process Anger

Let's look at a number of strategies that can be used to help you and your child process anger in a healthy way.

Defuse Angry Situations

Lindsey and her four kids had just completed a morning of shopping and errands. On the way home, they decided to pick up some lunch. As they drove to McDonald's, however, eight-year-old Chad began to throw a fit. "I want to go to Pizza Hut!" he howled over and over.

"We're going to McDonald's. It's on the way," Lindsey told him.

"I want to go to Pizza Hut! I want to go to Pizza Hut!"

Chad was yelling louder when the car pulled up to a stoplight. Suddenly he opened the door, jumped out of the car, and started running down the street. Lindsey was frantic. Chad was in an unfamiliar area, and she was concerned about his safety. But she had younger children in the car and couldn't leave them. And besides, she didn't want to give in to his outburst.

She took several deep breaths and waited. Finally, through the rearview mirror, she saw Chad inching back toward the car, obviously more curious about her lack of response than repentant.

Chad got in the car without a word, still seething. Lindsey managed to hold her own anger and said, "Are you all right?" She knew that confronting her son at that moment would only escalate his anger. She decided to drive straight home. No fast food today!

Lindsey's controlled response helped defuse her son's anger and kept the scene from becoming worse than it already was. Later, once everyone had calmed down, she was able to discuss Chad's misconduct with him rationally and administer appropriate consequences.

Divert the Anger

If she had thought about it, Lindsey could have used a different strategy: She could have anticipated Chad's anger and diverted it

123

before it was full blown. She knew Chad was hungry and a very picky eater. She also knew they'd been out shopping for several hours, and everyone was a bit cranky. While she might not have expected Chad to jump out of the car, it was probably a safe bet that he was going to cause some kind of commotion. "Momma's kitchen" might have been the best option from the start.

With some kids, it's better to anticipate and divert an explosive scenario *now* than to demand obedience later, when the child's anger is full-blown and he or she is bent on winning at all costs. Never argue with a kid who's drunk on power! Both of you may say or do things you'll regret. Better to stop the avalanche before it starts.

> *With some kids, it's better to anticipate and divert an explosive scenario* now *than to demand obedience later, when the child's anger is full-blown and he or she is bent on winning at all costs.*

The first step in diverting anger is determining *when* your child has a tendency to become angry. For example, does your preschooler frequently throw tantrums on Wednesdays and Fridays? Maybe it's because the two of you have an overly busy schedule on Tuesdays and Thursdays. If that's the case, cut back on Tuesday/Thursday activities, or provide for longer naps and quieter activities on Wednesdays and Fridays. Once you know when your child's buttons tend to get pushed, you can think of ways to get around those times without a blowup.

Older children can learn to divert their own anger. During a period of calm, help your child identify personal "warning signs" that indicate he or she is about to lose control—things like clenched fists or increased voice volume. Then brainstorm activities that he or she can do when those signs show up: jog around the block, play basketball, listen to music, journal, maybe go to a "think spot" under a tree in the yard. One parent taught her son to do deep-breathing techniques. They helped!

When the child notices the warning signs, he or she can begin immediately to jog, shoot hoops, write, breathe—whatever. And afterward, when the warning signs are gone, the two of you can discuss and hopefully resolve the issue that set off the warnings in the first place. Be sure to give your child kudos for handling the anger in an appropriate way.

Give Some Space

Many of the activities we listed above work because they give a child *space*. Sometimes children need a little space when they're angry, and that's OK. Closed doors are OK. We used to feel, when one of our boys went in his room and closed the door, that he was closing us out of his life. We took it personally. But then we realized that everyone needs space occasionally—even the little people in our lives. The *where* isn't important. When the daughter of one of our friends needed space, she'd go outside and sit in her dog's house!

Just for Parents

Believe us, we know how hard it is to deal with the anger of a spirited, strong-willed child. We've lived through our share of avalanches! But we've also discovered that the principles we've been discussing in this chapter really work.

We want to add two more vital principles especially for parents. The first one is, *Give your child a clean slate every day.* Here's what one mother of a spirited twelve-year-old told us:

> I've had to realize that I am the adult in this situation. My daughter is struggling with growing up. She's having a really hard time, and I want to love her, support her, and if

possible, make her road a little less bumpy. So each morning when I get up, I choose to give my daughter a clean slate. I throw away all the hurts from the day before. She's having a hard enough time—she doesn't need my extra baggage from yesterday. This helps me love and accept her one day at a time.

Perhaps you, like this mom, have "extra baggage" that you've been carrying with you from day to day—an accumulation of little hurts and frustrations that you need to release and throw away. Give your child a clean slate! Forgive, love, and accept your child one day at a time. That way, you'll be better able to help your child process anger, develop responsibility, and move toward maturity.

The second principle is, *Rely on prayer*. During the years our children were growing up, we kept a prayer diary for each of our boys. We found that when we gave our concerns to God in prayer and wrote them down, we didn't get as upset or nag our kids as much. We put the problems in God's hands—which meant we didn't have to keep worrying about them! Then, when we saw God answer our prayers for our sons, we recorded the answers in the diary too. Now we can look back over the years and see how gracious God has been to us.

Taking Steps toward a Better Future

Here are some practical things that you can do to help your spirited child—and all the members of your family—learn to deal with anger and frustration in appropriate ways:

Use the Anger Ladder

Discuss the anger ladder from pages 119–20 with your child during a peaceful time (not in the middle of a tantrum). Talk about a recent episode of anger and ask:

- "Which rung do you think you're on?"
- "Which rung do you *want* to be on?"
- "What do you need to do to get there?"

Have a Family Discussion

Get the whole family together and have each member discuss the answers to three questions:

1. What makes me angry?
2. What makes me frustrated?
3. What am I fearful of?

It can be as instructive for each member to hear one another's answers as it is to think through their own responses.

Keep an Anger Diary

After an episode in which you got angry, make a record of it in an "Anger Notebook." Record things like what made you angry, how you felt, and what you did. If you're not happy with the way you handled your anger, include what you *wish* you had done and what you would like to do the next time a similar situation comes up.

Do a Bible Study

Get family members together to discuss (and perhaps memorize) scriptures that have to do with the appropriate processing of anger. Here are three to start with:

1. "Be quick to listen, slow to speak, and slow to become angry." (James 1:19)

2. "The LORD is compassionate and gracious, slow to anger, abounding in love." (Ps. 103:8)

3. "'In your anger do not sin': Do not let the sun go down while you are still angry, and do not give the devil a foothold." (Eph. 4:26–27)

Make an "Alternatives to Hitting" List

Does your child hit, kick, or react in a violent way when he or she gets angry? During a calm time, ask your child to help you make an "Alternatives to Hitting (or Kicking, or...) List." Hang it on the refrigerator or other prominent place, and review it with your child from time to time. Jean Illsley Clarke, author of *Self-Esteem: A Family Affair,* suggests these alternatives for the list:[2]

- Take time to ask yourself what you want and/or need.
- Go outside and shoot hoops with a basketball.
- Punch a beanbag chair.
- Count to ten loudly in an angry voice. (Count to twenty if you need to.)
- Do an angry dance.
- Throw rocks in a lake or river.
- Pull some weeds in the yard.
- Blow into a paper bag and then pop the bag.
- Rip up old newspapers or magazines.
- Decide to think. Resolve the issues you're angry about.

Make an Anger Contract

Write out the following anger contract and discuss it with your family.

If everyone agrees to abide by it, have them sign it, and give each person a copy.

Anger Contract

- I will tell my family when I am getting angry.
- I will not attack other family members or vent my anger on them.
- I will ask for help in resolving whatever is making me angry.

— Set an Appointment

We sometimes resolved conflict and processed anger in our family by scheduling appointments with our children to discuss and work through specific issues. This gave us and our kids time and space to calm down, think through the situation, and prepare for the appointment. Ideally, our meeting took place within twenty-four hours of a blowup.

During the appointment time, we followed these four common-sense steps:

1. State the problem and each person's contribution to it.

2. Brainstorm and list possible solutions.

3. Choose a possible plan of action.

4. Try it. If it doesn't work, try another plan from the list.

— Adopt a Family Motto

Come up with a family motto, and display it in a prominent place. It could be something like, "In our family we build each other up. Others will tear us down."

Or, "In our family we attack problems, not each other!"

Getting Started Today

Anger is a powerful emotion. Even the best of us, when we're angry, do and say things that we really don't mean—and we're adults! So why should we expect our children, especially the more spirited ones, to have the self-control and the know-how to handle their anger in appropriate ways? We need to understand that when they cry, "I hate you!" they really mean, "I don't know what to do with my frustration and anger. Please help me!"

Teaching children to process their anger in a mature, responsible way takes lots of time and patience on our part. It takes us learning to process our own anger and then setting a good example. And it takes all of us—parents and children alike—looking to our ultimate example, God, who is always slow to anger and abounding in amazing love.

CRY #7

"I don't
Want To!"

What it really means:
"Give me the opportunity to develop responsibility."

My job was critical to the whole operation. The duties were complicated. The hours were long. Interpersonal relationships were touchy.

I (Claudia) was the "shower coordinator."

Let me explain. When we moved back to the United States after living in Germany and Austria for many years, we were all delighted to have more than one bathroom in our home. Mornings would be much simpler, we figured. Everyone in our family preferred showers, and we all wanted them in the morning—not at night. In our new house, that would be no problem, right?

But there *was* a problem. It wasn't the bathrooms; we had three of them. The problem was the water heater, of which we had only one. Thus, my job as shower coordinator. Each Arp could have no more than a couple of minutes in the shower, or our hot water would run out. (Too bad we didn't have a water heater like the one we had in Austria, which continually heated the water. But then I wouldn't have this story to tell.) My goal was to alleviate as much of the morning tension as possible and help everyone get out of the door on time. So each night I began negotiations for the next morning. Who should get up first? Who needed extra time? Who needed to get somewhere the earliest? The variables were many, and I coordinated them all.

Did it work? You've got to be kidding! On a typical cold winter morning, Kid Number One, who was supposed to be the first one in the shower, overslept. Kid Number Two got in instead, several minutes after the first shower should have begun. Then Kid Number One, realizing he was late, jumped in the shower next and let the water run too long. As a result, Kid Number Three had only cold water, and he didn't hesitate to let all of us know about it.

> An old adage says, "If you aim at nothing, you'll probably hit it." As parents, we need to set goals for our children now, while they're still under our roofs.

Naturally, our most spirited son had the hardest time dealing with the shower situation. He wanted to sleep late, take a long shower, and have plenty of hot water—just for him. As far as he was concerned, his brothers could take their showers at night. He wanted to do things himself, his own way—without having to concern himself with the needs of others.

One particularly hectic morning, Dave and I looked at each other in exasperation, and he said, "Why are you doing this? The boys aren't toddlers. They're in elementary and high school and old enough to work this one out on their own." After all, we agreed, who would coordinate their showers when they were in college or had families? Just who was learning responsibility now—the boys or the mom?

You may not be the shower coordinator at your house. But do you find yourself assuming other responsibilities for your kids? For example, do you stay on top of your fifteen-year-old daughter's homework assignments? After all, you wouldn't want her to turn a paper in late; it might bring down her grade. Do you remind your ten-year-old son to brush his teeth before going to bed? If you didn't, he would forget to brush, right? Do you put the dinner dishes in the dishwasher some nights, even though it's your twelve-year-old daughter's chore? You wouldn't want her to interrupt her phone call! Just who is learning self-discipline—you or your child?

We resolved the shower issue with three new alarm clocks and one brilliant statement: "Kids, you work it out!" Admittedly, we had a few harried mornings after that. But now the boys are grown, married, and have kids of their own; and as far as we know, they coordinate their own showers.

Understanding the Challenge

Children today are crying out for someone to teach them the responsibility and self-discipline they need, both now and in the future, to be successful in life. They don't say it in so many words, of course. We're more likely to hear, "I don't want to!" than, "Help me be responsible!" But *we* know what they really mean.

Future World

Take a trip into the future for a moment and picture yourself with your adult children. (Yes, even the spirited one will grow up eventually.) What kind of relationship would you like to have with each of them? What kind of relationship would you like for them to have with each other? Can you imagine having good times together, talking, laughing, appreciating one another? Wouldn't it feel good to enjoy your children—especially your spirited child—without feeling responsible for their lives?

The question is, how are you and your kids going to get to that idyllic point? An old adage says, "If you aim at nothing, you'll probably hit it." As parents, we need to set goals for our children now, while they're still under our roofs. What do they need to know about life before leaving home at eighteen or twenty? Will they be ready to function in the adult world? Get themselves up on time in the morning? Do the laundry so they have something clean to wear? Manage a checking account? Start a savings plan? Get along with bosses, coworkers, in-laws, and others?

They'll need to be able to do all these things and more! But ultimately, the lesson we need to teach them is not so much how to do this or that; it's how to be responsible and self-disciplined in all areas of life.

Here's how Jerry and Mary White, in their book *When Your Kids Aren't Kids Anymore*, expressed their goal for their children:

> Our overall goal for our sons and daughters is that they grow into mature, independent, godly adults who base their lives on sound principles, who are emotionally and spiritually strong, who have a strong sense of responsibility toward their fellow man, who will face good and difficult times with calmness and perseverance, and who, if married, become competent and faithful husbands, wives, and parents.[1]

Now there's a goal we can all adopt!

Out of Work and Loving It

The problem with being a parent is that by the time you are qualified for the job, you're unemployed. Before you know it, your kids are grown, and your work (for the most part) is done. But then, that's the point: to work yourself *out* of a job—and *into* a relationship that will last for a lifetime.

When the whole Arp gang gets together at our house, it's quite a scene. Between sons, daughters-in-law, and grandchildren, we number fifteen! We do a lot of talking and laughing, and we enjoy one another. But trust us, at this stage we have no control over our sons' lives. None. Zilch! We can offer guidance, but that's all. We've been worked out of our jobs—but not out of the relationships we nurtured over two wonderful, turbulent, hectic, happy decades of parenting.

Think about it: The relationship you're developing now is your link to your future relationship with your adult child—and with your grandkids! Someone jokingly said that the reason grandparents and grandchildren get along so well is that they have a common enemy between them. We take exception. Yes, teaching responsibility and self-discipline to kids, especially spirited ones, can be a real battle. But your child doesn't have to grow up to be your enemy!

By following the principles in this chapter, you can teach responsibility *and* build a strong, long-term relationship with your child based on mutual love and respect. The end result? You'll achieve your goal of sending a mature, responsible, caring young adult into the world. And what's more, you'll have a friend for life.

Dealing with the Present

The specific goals we have for our children can be broken down into two categories: who we want them to *be*, and what we want them to *do*.

The Goal of *Being*

Go back and look again at the goal written by Jerry and Mary White. At its core, it really has more to do with *internal virtues* than *external skills*. It's more about *being* than *doing*. Parents in our survey

135

identified these traits as the ones they wanted most to see developed in their kids:

- Concern for others
- Confidence
- Consideration
- Creativity
- Empathy
- Ethics
- Honesty
- Morality
- Responsibility
- Spirituality

What values and virtues do you want to nurture in your child? (If you're having trouble making a list, read through God's lists in Galatians 5; 1 Corinthians 13; and 2 Peter 1.) After identifying those values you'd like to see developed, think about what each one would look like in your child's life. Then ask:

- What am I doing right now to help my child develop this quality?
- Am I modeling this virtue and reinforcing it by my example?
- What can I do from this point on to nurture this virtue in my child's life?

The Goal of *Doing*

Think about this question: What does your child need to know how to do by the time he or she moves out of the house? What will your child be personally responsible for when he or she is an independent young adult? Take a few moments to make a list.

Now think about how that list can be broken down and fleshed out at different age levels or stages. Starting at your child's age, you might want to complete the following sentences:

- When my son (or daughter) is two, he should be able to....
- When he enters preschool, he should be able to....
- When he's a first grader, he should be able to....
- When he starts middle school, he should be able to....
- When he becomes a teenager, he should be able to....
- When he leaves home, he should be able to....

What are reasonable expectations to have for different ages and stages? In the box on the next page, you'll see a breakdown of age-appropriate responsibilities suggested by Jean Lush in her book *Mothers and Sons* for children age two through sixth grade. As your child moves on through middle school and high school, your expectations should rise accordingly. Each year you should be able to give duties and encourage capabilities in your son or daughter that involve increasing amounts of maturity, responsibility, and freedom.

Hands off Homework!

Notice that one of the age-appropriate responsibilities a child in sixth grade should be able to master is scheduling time for studies. This leads to an important issue: schoolwork.

Some parents go overboard trying to help their children succeed academically. They push their kids through school, feeling so responsible for their children's achievement that the children never take responsibility for their own academic success. The result? When the kids go off to college, they fall apart academically because they don't have their parents there to monitor their work and help them with their studies.

Age-Appropriate Responsibilities[2]		
Ages Two to Four	**Ages Four to Five**	**Ages Five to Six**
• Pick up toys and put them away • Clean up dropped food • Choose between two foods at breakfast • Make simple decisions • Do simple hygiene—brush teeth, wash and dry hands and face	• Set the table • Help put groceries away • Feed pets on a schedule • Dust the furniture	• Help with the meal planning and grocery shopping • Make own sandwich or simple breakfast, then clean up • Make bed • Clean room
First Grade	**Second Grade**	**Third Grade**
• Choose clothes to wear • Water plants and flowers • Cook simple foods • Rake leaves and weeds	• Take care of bike • Take phone messages • Water the lawn • Wash the dog or cat	• Fold napkins and set silverware properly • Straighten closet and drawers • Shop for and select own clothes with parent's help • Follow recipes and do simple cooking
Fourth Grade	**Fifth Grade**	**Sixth Grade**
• Operate the washer and dryer • Prepare a simple family meal • Receive and answer own mail • Wait on a guest	• Be alone at home for short periods • Handle small sums of money • Take the city bus • Be responsible for a personal hobby	• Join outside organizations, do assignments, and attend meetings • Put siblings to bed and dress them • Mow lawn with supervision • Schedule time for studies

If you spend nearly all of your free time in the evening helping your kids with their homework, *don't!* That's the advice of Linda Sonna, author of *The Homework Solution: Getting Kids to Do Their Homework.* While it's probably wise to help your children study for big tests, and maybe even help them organize big projects, Sonna cautions parents from taking over routine homework responsibilities. This practice not only stunts the development of responsibility, it stunts achievement. Research shows that kids whose parents routinely help them with math and language homework score lower on achievement tests than kids whose parents offer no help.[3]

Keeping "hands off" isn't easy, especially when your spirited child balks at doing homework night after night. One mom told us, "With my difficult child, I can only help so much. When I cross the line, he heads straight for a meltdown. So a helpful strategy I've adopted is to let him live with the consequences. I simply say in a calm voice, 'It's your choice—you can do your homework and turn it in on time, or you can get a zero.'" The result is that her son has gotten much better at being responsible for his homework assignments!

Motivating Kids to Accept Responsibility

This mom's experience illustrates an important point: Identifying responsibilities that are age appropriate doesn't mean that spirited children will accept those responsibilities willingly. They have to be sufficiently motivated.

Whatever method you use to motivate your child, we recommend that you season it with *lots of positive feedback*. Often our tendency as parents is to focus more attention on our children's negative behavior than their positive behavior. We need to reverse that! When you catch your child being responsible, reinforce that positive behavior with praise—for example, "I'm so proud of you for putting your coat on the coat hook without being asked!"

One way to give feedback and provide motivation is to set up a point system that awards points to your child for good behavior—for example, fewer outbursts; showing kindness toward a sibling—and for completing assigned responsibilities, like making the bed or putting the dishes in the dishwasher after dinner. At the end of the week (or end of the month, if your child is older), he or she turns in the earned points in exchange for an award that the two of you have agreed upon—say, a trip to the ice cream store, a new toy, or a certain sum of money. To keep interest high, the awards should be changed frequently, and your child should have input into what they will be.

Many parents report good results from using this or similar reward systems. One parent who started giving out points in her home told us her children made positive changes much more rapidly than she had anticipated!

Be careful not to *de*-motivate your child by setting your expectations too high. And keep in mind that children—especially spirited ones—need transition time between their activities and their responsibilities. For example, if your seven-year-old son is building with Legos and it's almost time for him to set the table for dinner, give him a warning so he can make the emotional transition from fun to chores. One early childhood educator suggests giving a five-minute warning to kids age six and over and a two-minute warning for younger children. "This works at our house with our difficult daughter," she says. "But when I forget and don't give her a proper warning and transition time, she can go ballistic in no time flat!"

The Challenge of Chores

Motivating spirited children to accept responsibility around the house can be difficult, but the effort is worth it. Research shows that children who help at home with specific chores learn responsibility, gain self-esteem, and develop valuable work habits for their adult life.

To this end, we recommend that parents make a "chore chart" with their kids. This way, children know what is expected of them, and parents have a tool to gauge the follow-through. We've found that the secret to using charts effectively is to change them often. Consider making weekly charts, one-time charts, or checklists for different times of day. Here's an example:

> ## Morning Chart for Maria
>
> Before I leave for school this morning, I will:
>
> ✓ get up on time on my own
>
> ✓ get dressed
>
> ✓ make my bed
>
> ✓ eat breakfast
>
> ✓ brush my teeth
>
> ✓ comb my hair

If your child is very young and doesn't read yet, you can make a chart together using pictures that you draw or cut from magazines—photos or illustrations of people brushing their teeth, getting dressed, making the bed, and so on. When your child gets up in the morning, say, "Look at your chart. It will tell you what to do." The chart becomes the one "giving orders," not you!

With young children, you also can turn chores into games. Here are two you can play:

1. *Beat the Clock.* Set a timer for five minutes and challenge your child to "beat the clock" by completing the job before the buzzer rings.

2. *Do You Live Here?* With your child at your side, walk up to

something in the room and say, "Do you live here?" Then pretend the object answers you. For example, you could say to the coffee table, "Coffee table, do you live here?" The coffee table answers, "Yes." Then ask the ball on the floor, "Ball, do you live here?" Let your child answer for the ball: "No, I don't live here. I live in the toy box." Then let your child take the ball home to the toy box. Continue for as long as your child will participate and the game stays fun.

(We include more fun, motivational games and activities later in this chapter.)

House Rules

In addition to making a chore chart, we recommend developing a set of "house rules." And while it's best to have as few rules as possible and to say "yes" as often as possible, spirited children generally don't like surprises; it helps for them to have things clearly spelled out.

You can keep your rules to a minimum by asking, "Does this rule deal with a major issue?" If it doesn't, you may want to drop that rule or make it more flexible. Whatever rules you come up with, make sure your child knows what the consequences will be for non-compliance. A consequence should be age-appropriate, of course, and proportionate to the offense. For example, you might tell your five-year-old daughter, "If you don't pick up your toys, you won't get to watch a video this afternoon." Or you could say to your teenage son, "If you don't mow the lawn Saturday afternoon, you won't get to go with your friends to the soccer game Saturday night."

The following list of general house rules has been widely distributed, and for good reason. Any household could benefit from it! The author is unknown. You may want to make a copy and post the list on your refrigerator or in a prominent place:

House Rules

When I turn it on . . . . I turn it off.

When I unlock something . . . I lock it up.

When I drop something . . . . . I pick it up.

When I open something . . . . . I close it.

When I make a mess . . . . I clean it up.

When I make a promise . . . . . I keep my promise.

When I find something . . . . . I return it.

When I take it out . . . . I put it back.

When I am assigned a task . . . I complete it on time.

When I earn money . . . . I spend and invest it wisely.

What if your strong-willed son or daughter cries, "I didn't make those rules, and I won't keep them"? You may be tempted to respond, "Tough, I'm the parent!" But a more effective answer might be, "OK, let's discuss our family guidelines and negotiate them together." Discussing and negotiating the rules definitely takes more work, but sometimes spirited children are more willing to respect and cooperate with rules when they've had some input into them.

Learning to Be Responsible with Money

One lesson that's imperative for our children to learn before they leave home is how to be responsible with money. But as the old Chinese proverb says, "To manage money, you have to have some money." Our kids need to have at least a little money in their pockets—otherwise, what will they have to work with as we teach them good money management?

The Lessons of Allowance

Giving your child an allowance can be a great teaching tool. One early childhood specialist we know says that he sets his children's allowance aside in three parts:

- money for savings
- money for church (a tithe)
- money to spend with no rules attached

He also applies these rules:

- Each child must take his own money to the store.
- Parents will not loan money that the child forgot to bring.
- Getting money out of savings must be done ahead of time.

What if the children spend their "free" money foolishly? That's OK, he says. Gradually, through their foolish financial decisions, they will learn to be more self-disciplined and to spend their money in more reasonable ways.

Learning through Earning

Another great way to teach children about the value of money and good money management is to encourage them to earn some. Why not have a brainstorming session with your child and make a list of age-appropriate jobs he or she might be interested in pursuing? Here are some ideas one family came up with:

- Have a yard sale and get rid of old toys and clothes.
- Grow tomatoes and cucumbers to sell to neighbors.
- Do yard work (mow grass, pull weeds, plant flowers).
- Water plants for neighbors on a regular basis.
- Teach younger children a sport or skill.

- Provide entertainment for birthday parties.

- Baby-sit.

- Take care of other people's pets when they are out of town.

- Walk dogs.

- Clean and organize attics and garages.

When we lived in Vienna, Austria, our three sons created their own peanut butter business. Every week they bought peanuts, made peanut butter, and sold it to families in Vienna and also to missionaries in Hungary and Poland who would come to Vienna from time to time. They became known as the Arp Peanut Butter Brothers, and their business motto was "One hundred percent pure peanut butter—we're all nuts for you!"

The boys kept track of the cost of the peanuts, the number of jars sold, the number of hours they worked, and so on. The profit was divided between them, based on the amount of time each one invested in the business. Of course, as parents and supervisors, we put many of our own hours into the enterprise. We even pitched in with the clean-up sometimes. But our sons learned so many valuable financial lessons that we considered it time well spent.

The truth is, helping our children develop responsibility is always a lot of work for parents—whether the lesson is good money management or putting toys back in the toy box. But the rewards are great. The responsibility and self-discipline our children learn from us now will benefit them the rest of their lives.

Taking Steps toward a Better Future

Just because helping your child develop responsibility is hard doesn't mean it can't be fun—for both of you! Here are some games and activities to try. We include appropriate ages for each activity, but your child's response is really the best guide. If you think your child will like a particular game, go for it!

Play Pick-up Games

The following games are great for getting kids to help clean or pick up around the house:

- *The President Is Coming*—Pretend the president is coming to your house for dinner. What needs to be done before he gets there? (preschool to seven years old)

- *Zone Offense*—Divide the house into zones, with each family member keeping an area clean. Then have a contest and give an award to the person with the cleanest zone. (preschool with supervision to ten-years-old)

- *The Job Jar*—Designate a "job jar." Write various jobs that need to be done on slips of paper and place them in the job jar. Have each person draw for his or her task. For difficult tasks, assign job teams. (all ages)

- *Alphabet Pick-up*—This is a variation of the "Do You Live Here?" game we mentioned earlier in the chapter. Ask your child to find out-of-place items that begin with different sounds or letters of the alphabet; for example: "Can you find something that needs to be picked up that begins with a B sound?" Your child might find the book on the couch that needs to be returned to the bookshelf. (preschool and early elementary)

- *Pick Up Ten in Ten*—Have each child pick up exactly ten things and put them away in ten minutes' time. If you have three children, that means thirty items will be picked up in about ten minutes! (preschool and early elementary)

Play the Give, Earn, Save, Spend Game

This is a great way to teach kindergarten and early elementary-age kids about the value and management of money. Write the words *Give, Earn, Save,* and *Spend* on separate index cards and give a set to each family member. Then suggest situations that could involve giving, earning, saving, or spending. For example:

- Your grandparents gave you fifty dollars for Christmas.
- Your best friend's birthday is next week.
- Your church is putting together food baskets for needy families.
- Your favorite movie just came out on video.
- You got five dollars for cleaning out the garage.

Have the other family members hold up the card that best describes their initial response to the statement. Would they give, earn, save, or spend in that situation? Discuss the responses. Consider: What are the advantages of giving, earning, saving, or spending in each situation?

Teach How the Ants Do It

Kindergarten and elementary-aged children can learn a lot about the importance of self-discipline, hard work, and saving by observing the work habits of ants. Purchase an ant farm from a local hobby store or track a busy ant colony in your backyard. Say, "Do you see how the ants are carrying bits of food? They're working hard, aren't they? Where are the ants taking the food? What do you think they'll eat in the winter when it's cold and they can't find food?"

Read Proverbs 30:25 aloud: "Ants are creatures of little strength, yet

147

they store up their food in the summer." Then make an ant poster with your child using felt pens, pictures, or drawings. Write the Bible verse on it, or make your own paraphrase: "Remember the ants—save a dollar for later!"

▬ Do Back-to-School Shopping

When shopping for school clothes or supplies with a child in third or fourth grade or above, announce the amount you are willing to spend. Then let your child decide what items to purchase within that limit. This teaches them how to prioritize their needs and wants and how to stay within a budget. It's also good math practice!

▬ Develop a Chore Chart and House Rules

Go back in this chapter and read about the usefulness of chore charts and the importance of house rules. Work with your child to develop both.

Getting Started Today

Gene Bedley, a school principal and a father of three, understands the importance of teaching responsibility to kids. He says, "What really serves children is helping them understand how to respond to the world. Responsibility can be simply defined as my ability to respond. Encouraging responsibility amounts to helping a child see cause and effect. The bottom line of what responsibility means is this: I come to a place in my life where I acknowledge what I do."[4]

Teaching responsibility and self-discipline—especially to a strong-willed or spirited child—is not easy. But it's worth all the effort we put into it. The end result is what we all want: children who have grown into responsible young adults, equipped with all the tools necessary to navigate successfully through the rest of their lives.

CRY #8

"I'm *a big kid* Already!"

What it really means:
"Guide me to maturity."

Eleven-year-old Tiffany was dead serious when she announced to her mother: "If I had my driver's license and could drive a car, I could live in an apartment on my own. I really don't need parents anymore."

We've known Tiffany since she was a baby, and we can vouch that she's a certified spirited kid who is eleven going on twenty-one. Fortunately, she has a mom who understands the challenge, having previously parented Tiffany's strong-willed older sister (who is now married, through medical school, and expecting her first child). It was really no surprise that both girls turned out to be spirited. As a child, Tiffany's mom had been strong-willed—and research shows that parents who were strong-willed as children tend to have kids with similar temperaments.

"Tiffany has never been one to go with the flow," her mother tells us. "She has always had a real intensity about life. When she wants something, she doesn't budge. And she definitely has a very independent spirit. I think she honestly believes she could do just fine on her own!

"It helps to realize that this is just for a season, and that Tiffany's strong-willed traits will help her be a more secure and confident adult," she says. "My daughter will never just 'follow the crowd.' She will definitely seek out her own path. I just want to do everything I can to point her in the right direction!"

How can we, as parents, guide spirited children like Tiffany to maturity? After all, they're convinced that they're big kids already! How can we work ourselves out of a constant, hands-on parenting job and into a mature relationship with our spirited children that spans a lifetime?

Understanding the Challenge

Parenting a spirited child to maturity definitely presents a greater challenge than parenting a more compliant child. While the compliant child is usually flexible and tends to cooperate, the spirited child is more rigid and uncooperative. While the easy-going child readily accepts discipline; the strong-willed child resists. While the compliant child can usually handle strong emotions with only an occasional blowup, the difficult child has one meltdown after another.

Since spirited, difficult children are just that—spirited and difficult—we need more of everything to guide them to maturity: more patience, more energy, more unconditional love, more trust, more humor. We need more faith that God has a plan for our children's lives—especially as we give up increasing degrees of control and responsibility as our kids approach adulthood.

It may sound funny to say, but losing control is what parenting is really all about. We're *supposed* to lose control. The challenge is to lose control in a controlled manner, little by little, letting go of the right amount at the right time.

When our spirited son was twelve years old, he told us, "Mom, Dad, I don't want to learn from the *experienced*. I want to learn by *experience!*"

Those are scary words for a parent to hear. But the fact is, "by experience" is often the way spirited, strong-willed children learn best. I remember the time our son saved his money to buy a Walkman and insisted on taking it on a school ski trip. Yep, he came home minus one Walkman. It had been stolen. It was a hard lesson, but the next time he went on a school trip, he left his valuables at home.

We can't give our kids paradise. We can't protect them from the pain and suffering of life. (A friend of ours, a clinical psychologist, said that his goal for his kids was "to get them to adulthood with as little damage as possible.") But we *can* coach them through a training program that will build the "maturity muscles" they'll need to carry adult burdens in the future.

Dealing with the Present

If your spirited child is determined to learn by experience, how can you provide the framework he or she needs to learn positive life lessons in the process? One way is to teach your child good decision-making skills.

From an early age, kids need to be given opportunities to make their own decisions. No, you can't allow a ten-year-old to choose his or her own bedtime. But there are some things that are safe for children at various ages and stages to decide for themselves.

One mom told us that when her son turned eight, she decided he was old enough to begin choosing the clothes he wore to school. "That was a real challenge for me, because I care about how my son looks and what other people think," she said. "Would you believe he chose to wear the same jeans—the ones with a hole in the knee—every day for a year? I washed them often, so they were clean; but I was the only one who knew that. To make matters worse, he was a safety patrol officer, which meant he opened car doors for kids being dropped off in the morning and picked up in the afternoon. Most of the mothers in the school knew him and saw him every day!

"Was I embarrassed? Yes! Did it improve our relationship? Yes. Did my friends ask me why I didn't buy my son a new pair of jeans? Yes. Still, I'm glad I honored our agreement and kept his clothes as his own decision."

Helping Kids Make Decisions

Being able to make wise, independent decisions is a key to successful adult living. That's why it's so important for us to involve our children in the decision-making process as often as possible. Here are four tips that helped us teach decision making to our sons:

1. Allow your child to participate in family decisions.

Whether it's deciding what television program you are going to watch as a family, what game you are going to play, or where you're going on a family vacation, let your children take part. This builds their confidence in their own decision-making abilities. If you're planning a family vacation, let an older child research several possible destinations, routes, plane fares, accommodations, and points of interest. The Internet is a great place to do research, and your child is probably more proficient at navigating the Internet than you are!

2. Let your child choose between options.

Even young children can make simple decisions like, "Do you want the red apple or the green one?" "Do you want to brush your teeth with the green toothpaste or the striped toothpaste?" "Do you want to take your nap in your bed or on the couch in the playroom?" Giving choices on simple matters helps your child develop his or her ability to analyze options.

If your child asks, "Why do I have to wear a coat?" you can turn the question into a decision-making opportunity. Say, "What is the weather like outside today? Is it hot or cold? Do you think the light red coat would be warm enough, or would the heavy blue coat feel better?"

3. Encourage your child to negotiate.

This tip may not excite you, since your spirited son or daughter is probably a natural-born debater. But when you have an issue to work through with your child, it's a good idea to walk through the four steps of negotiation that we discussed in a previous chapter:

- Let your child summarize what he or she wants.
- Summarize what you want.
- Propose alternatives.
- Work out a compromise.

Negotiating with a strong-willed kid can take lots of time and effort. It's so much simpler to say, "Do this" or "Don't do that." But when you take the easy route, how are you training your child to become a competent decision maker? (Never mind the fact that he or she probably hates being told what to do.)

4. Expect your child to make some inappropriate decisions.

The hardest part of teaching decision making is watching your child make mistakes. Let's say your nine-year-old son receives money for his birthday, and he's determined to spend it on a toy that he saw on television—one that you know he'll be bored with in a week. Should you allow him to buy the toy and learn the hard lesson of spending money unwisely? Most of us learn more through our mistakes than through our successes, and the same is true for our kids. Sometimes we just have to bite our tongues and our tendency to control and keep hands off. As one parent said, "You hope and pray that when your child makes a mistake, he or she will have an excellent learning opportunity, and your tendency to nag will be stifled."

Of course, allowing children—especially spirited children—the freedom to make wrong decisions can be hard, if not downright embarrassing. We may feel great when our son or daughter is the star of the soccer team or everyone's darling, but it's not as much fun being known as "the father of the boy with the weird haircut" or "the mother of the girl who just blew her entire allowance at the cosmetic counter so she could look like a Barbie doll."

Hang in there! The more we help our children develop confidence and competence in making decisions on minor issues (hairstyles, clothes, and so on), the less likely they'll be to rebel and make bad choices when it comes to major things like drugs, alcohol, and sex. If we do the hard work now, by the time they are selecting colleges and mates and making their own moral choices, we'll be able to breathe a little easier knowing their decision-making skills are well-developed.

Challenging Children to Grow

Strong-willed, spirited children have a natural desire to control their own lives. Yet, precisely because they can be difficult, we tend to strip them of control just when they yearn for it the most—for example, as they move into adolescence. A better course is to turn that yearning into motivation to grow. Spirited kids don't respond well to ultimatums, but they do respond to challenges. Challenging them to move on to the next level of maturity—and the next level of responsibility and freedom—can be an effective motivational tool.

The summer before each of our sons turned thirteen, we gave them a four-part challenge to help them prepare for the teenage years. We challenged them in four areas: physical, intellectual, spiritual, and practical. The physical challenge was to run a mile in under eight minutes. The intellectual challenge was to read a book about someone they admired and give a book report to the whole family. The spiritual challenge was to complete a Bible study teaching a biblical code of conduct and to commit to abide by that code through their teen years. For the practical challenge, they planned a campout with me (Dave) and did all the work involved, including cooking all the meals. (Yes, I ate some very interesting things!)

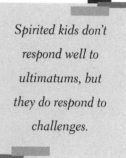

Spirited kids don't respond well to ultimatums, but they do respond to challenges.

You may be thinking, "My child would *never* cooperate with something like that!" But he or she just might go along with the right motivation. Some children can be motivated simply by the knowledge that you're looking to see if they're ready for expanded responsibilities and privileges; others may need the addition of something more tangible. For example, one of our sons was less than excited about doing his teenage challenge—that is, until we made the reward the new skis he really wanted.

A teenage challenge is a great initiation into the teen years. It helps to ensure that your child enters this often turbulent phase of life with increased confidence and self-assurance. But challenges can be a motivation to greater maturity at every age and stage of your child's growth. Your preschooler can be challenged to learn how to tie his or her shoes before entering kindergarten, for example. Your fifth grader can be challenged to set the alarm clock and get up in the morning without your assistance before starting middle school.

Involve your child in the design of some of the challenges. You'll be surprised at how creative and helpful the input can be. Besides, your spirited child is likely to be more cooperative if he or she feels some ownership of the idea. Make sure the challenges are simple, achievable, and measurable, and include a celebration or reward at their completion. We include more ideas for age-related challenges at the end of the chapter.

Letting Go and Letting God

As our children get older, our role in their lives needs to change from that of *director* to *facilitator* and then *observer*. Scary as it seems, our children must make the jump from living by our family rules and standards to living by their own personal convictions. They must move from dependence on us, the parents, to dependence on God. And it's our job to help them.

Unfortunately, this transition is not a science. There are no ten easy steps to helping kids grow spiritually. When they're young, we can read them Bible stories and teach simple Bible verses. Later, we can encourage quiet-time notebooks and check-up charts. We can pray with and for our children. We can involve them in sending supplies to missionaries and giving assistance to the needy. We can teach by example. But as much as we'd like to legislate spiritual growth and maturity, we can't.

Earlier in the book we stated that spirited children will make an impact on this world—one way or another. There are no guarantees that, as young adults, they will choose to make their impact based on our convictions. We can influence, but we cannot control. Ultimately, their faith must be internalized and their convictions must be their own. We can only do what we can do—and put the rest in God's hands.

A belief must be chosen freely. But children are not free to choose God's way as their own until they're given the choice. What if your son or daughter begins to struggle with questions about the faith you've taught? Admittedly, that can be hard to swallow. But a child who wrestles with his or her beliefs is, in many ways, healthier than one who never struggles because he or she is never given the gift of personal choice. The child who is never given a choice leaves home equipped only with a habit of conforming to parental standards—and no strong convictions of his or her own.

When that child is thrust into a whole new world, with all kinds of new philosophies and lifestyles clamoring for attention, he or she has no parental influence to provide the moral compass. The result is likely to be confusion and heartache. How much better for a child to form basic convictions while still at home!

We encourage you to start planning and working *now* to shift the responsibility for your child's spiritual life from your shoulders to your child's. Here are some suggestions for beginning that shift:

- *Encourage your spirited child to ask questions.* Most families have at least one resident cynic, and we were no exception. Sometimes our boys asked questions that really surprised us. While we did not always have answers for every question, we tried to help our sons find the answers. Remember, kids today face hot issues in high school like abortion, AIDS, premarital sex, homosexuality, drugs and alcohol abuse, and more. If you don't help answer their questions, someone else surely will.

- *Provide good reading material and Christian music.* Whenever our children requested our help in purchasing good literature or music with Christian lyrics, we tried to help them.

- *Look for mentors.* Godly young adults can influence your child in positive ways. Church youth groups, Christian camps, and conferences are great places to find mentors for your teenager. (Mentors can be especially helpful during those years when parents seem to lose all their credibility with their own children.)

- *Be a good role model.* We can't say we were always great role models for our sons, but we tried to be. We weren't always consistent, but over the years we consistently tried to be!

- *Pray for your child.* Parenthood—even single parenthood—is not a solitary occupation. We have a partner with unlimited resources: the living God. Talk to him often about your child!

- *Trust God for what you don't yet see.* We were able to keep going during the hard times because we knew God was totally committed to us and to our family. Psalm 138:8 says, "The LORD will perfect that which concerns me" (NKJV). When you need hope for the future, remember verses such as Romans 8:25: "But if we hope for what we do not see, we eagerly wait for it with perseverance" (NKJV), and 1 Corinthians 9:10: "He who plows should plow in hope" (NKJV).

- *Choose to trust your child.* During the teen years especially, it can be difficult to trust your spirited child. When our sons were adolescents, we often had to make a conscious effort to *choose* to invest trust in them. They weren't perfect, and sometimes we got hurt. But ultimately each one proved himself worthy of our trust.

Counselor Norm Wright gives this advice:

> Trusting your teen means running the risk of having that trust broken. It might be nice if you could get your adolescent to promise in writing not to betray your trust; you could even get it notarized. But it would only be a piece of paper. As in any love relationship, you have to risk being hurt. You'll be disappointed, just as I've been at times. That's the price of saying "I still love you."[1]

Trust is something we invest and reinvest in our children. It's crucial to our relationship with them—and absolutely necessary for their growth and maturity. It's also necessary if we're ever going to let go of our control over their lives. And let go we must, at the right time, in the right way. After all, we're parents. That's our job.

Taking Steps toward a Better Future

Check out our book *Suddenly They're Thirteen* for information and suggestions on planning and carrying out a teenage challenge.[2] For younger kids, try some of these:

Adopt a Preschool Challenge

When you challenge your preschooler, be sure to make it fun. And while you should encourage your child to succeed, don't push him or her to excel. Pushing only adds to a preschooler's stress level—and stress is one thing we all can do with less of! Here are some things you can challenge your preschooler to learn:

- child and parent's full name
- address
- phone number
- ABC's
- basic numbers
- colors

Adopt an Elementary School Challenge

Good elementary school-age challenges include:

- Read a book and give an oral report to the family.
- Learn how to sort the dirty clothes and operate the washer and dryer.
- Memorize several Bible verses.
- Learn a new computer skill.
- Keep a journal for a period of time.
- Make a dessert for the whole family.
- Write letters to grandparents or cousins.

Do a Proverbs Bible Study

As a family, read and discuss what the Book of Proverbs has to say about these negative behaviors:

- Running with the wrong crowd (Prov. 1:10–19)
- Lying (Prov. 14:5; 19:9)
- Laziness (Prov. 13:4; 20:4; 24:30–34)

- Sexual immorality (Prov. 5; 6:24–35)
- Losing temper (Prov. 14:17, 29; 19:19; 20:3)
- Jealousy (Prov. 14:30)
- Offending a brother (Prov. 18:19)
- Disobeying parents (Prov. 13:1; 15:5)

▬ Encourage Hope

Using a good concordance, make a list of all the Bible verses containing the word *hope*. When you feel discouraged, read through some of these verses. Remind yourself that your hope is in a faithful and trustworthy God.

Getting Started Today

We remember reading a newspaper column by the late humorist Erma Bombeck many years ago. In it she gave a great word picture of what it means to "let go" as we lead our children to maturity. She likened a child to a kite and a parent to the person at the other end of the string, trying to get the kite off the ground. The parent runs until he or she is breathless; the kite crashes. The parent adds a longer tail; the kite ends up in the drain spout. Still the parent keeps patching, adjusting, and working with the kite, confident that one day it will fly.

Finally the kite is airborne, and the parent lets out a little more string…and a little more…and a little more. The kite continues to rise higher, becoming more distant with each twist of the ball of twine. Then, with a deep sigh, the parent lets go, and the kite soars as it was meant to soar, independent and free.

Letting out string is risky. Finally releasing that string is riskier still. But that's the ultimate goal of parenting: to guide our spirited children to the point where, like kites, they can soar successfully on their own.

Are you afraid that when you finally let go, you'll be empty-handed? You won't! What you'll have left is the relationship you've built with your child through the active parenting years. As two parents who managed to release three soaring sons, let us encourage you: The joy of seeing your precious kite rise on the wind, full of purpose and grace, is worth all the risks. And your relationship with your adult child—not to mention any grandchildren he or she may produce—will have its own rewards.

Maintaining *your* Parental Sanity

For eight chapters we've been focusing on your spirited son or daughter. In this concluding chapter, we want to focus on *you*, the parent. How can you maintain your sanity and live a balanced life while parenting a child that presents a constant challenge? How can you find encouragement and support?

It's not uncommon for parents of spirited kids to experience parental burnout. If you're parenting alone or you're a mom working outside the home, your risk is even higher. To see if you're a candidate for burnout, check for these symptoms:

- You're living life faster and enjoying it less.
- You haven't had lunch with a friend in months.
- You keep telling yourself, "Things will slow down tomorrow."
- You don't have any energy and get up each morning feeling exhausted.
- You tend to expect negative behavior from your spirited child.
- You can't remember the last time you got some exercise.
- You lost your temper again and said things you regret.

- You have a lingering cold, backache, or _____ (you fill in the blank) that just won't go away.
- You think dating is something you and your spouse did before you had kids.
- You go to sleep and wake up thinking about your "problem child."

No doubt you could add to our list—but don't exhaust yourself further by thinking about it! The important question is, how can you regroup and get re-energized once you've hit the wall?

Here are seven steps you can take to overcome burnout and avoid it in the future:

1. Take stock of your life.

Make a list of the things that you do on a regular basis that end up causing you the most pressure and stress. (You might want to keep a "burnout log" for a couple of weeks to make sure you don't miss anything.) Which of the things on the list aren't really necessary and can be dropped from your schedule? Which can be done by someone besides you? Parents are not bionic; we're not angels who need neither food nor sleep. We can only do so much before the accumulated stress of all that we do pushes us over the top.

2. Don't overcommit.

Make sure you ask yourself three questions before accepting any new responsibilities that could end up in your burnout log:

- How much will it cost me in time and energy?
- If I accept this new responsibility, can I stop doing something I am presently doing?
- Does this activity advance my personal goals?

3. Stop worrying.

Parenting spirited kids can be a scary undertaking. Whenever we feel responsible for things that aren't completely in our control (like our strong-willed children), we can't help but get anxious. The older our children are, the less we can control, and the more things we find to worry about! You can overcome your tendency to worry and fret by remembering these keys:

- *Don't obsess over your mistakes.* It's not our mistakes that hurt our children; it's our bad attitudes. The attitude that says, "I'm the parent, so I'm always right; and you're the child, so you're always wrong," is deadly. We all make mistakes! We just need to be willing to admit them.

- *Apologize when you blow it.* We're sure our sons learned how to ask for forgiveness by our modeling it to them over and over. We made it a habit to go back to them and say, "Please forgive me. I was wrong to yell at you." "I didn't really listen to you." "I judged you unfairly." As a result, our sons were always willing to forgive us. They knew they didn't have perfect parents, but they never traded us in. Today they are among our best *friends*.

- *Take time out.* Remember to get enough sleep and rest—you're not an angel! If you have to, hire a sitter to take your children to the park while you take a nap.

- *Have a sense of humor.* Laughing at ourselves helps us relax. If joking comes naturally in your home, you're fortunate! Some families are natural cut-ups, while others have to work at keeping the atmosphere light. In our home we placed cartoons and jokes on the refrigerator door for everyone to enjoy. We tried to look for the humor in every situation, even the heavy or irritating ones.

- *Don't hesitate to get outside help.* It's important to recognize that some problems are deeper than others. We can do everything right, yet our children can have serious problems like ADHD, chronic depression, drug abuse, and eating disorders that are beyond our ability to resolve. If that's the case in your home, you need to seek outside help. You can start with your own pastor. If necessary, the church can direct you to a qualified Christian counselor or mental health professional.

- *Don't wallow in guilt.* Ultimately our children must live their own lives and accept responsibility for their own behavior. Yes, we should love them, guide them, pray for them, and never give up hope. But if they make bad choices, we shouldn't allow ourselves to wallow in guilty feelings. After all, there are no perfect parents and no perfect children this side of heaven. Even God has rebellious children, and he *is* the perfect parent!

4. Prepare for the future.

If your child is just starting preschool, you may find this hard to believe: You won't be parenting your spirited child for the rest of your life! Trust us, there is life after the kids grow up and leave home, and you should begin now to prepare for it.

Over the years we've observed many parents who were so focused on their children's lives that they forgot about nurturing their own. When their children grew up and moved out, all of their energy and

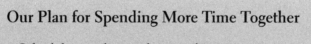

vitality was sucked out with them. The parents found themselves rambling around in a house that was suddenly too big, trying to relate to a spouse they no longer really knew. No wonder so many marriages break up during the empty nest years! Now—while you're still in the parenting years—is the time to prepare for your future.

5. Set goals.

We would all probably agree on certain goals in life: to love and nurture our children; to influence our world positively; if married, to love and support our spouse. But quite often our goals are too numerous, too general, or too difficult to measure to be of any real value in our day-to-day lives.

When we lead our Marriage Alive Seminars, we try to help couples set realistic, workable goals for their marriage. We suggest that their goals meet three criteria: They must be specific; they must be measurable; and they should cover a time frame.

Let's say a couple decides on the general goal of spending more time together so they can work on building a closer relationship. Their actual plan might look something like this:

Our Plan for Spending More Time Together

- Schedule one date night a week.
- Walk together for thirty minutes after dinner three times each week.
- Plan a weekend away together in the next two months.
- Read one book on communication in marriage and discuss it within the next month.

If you're a single parent, your goals should be specific and measurable too. Let's say you have a general goal of building a support system for yourself and your child. (We strongly recommend it!) Specifically, you might find other parents who have spirited children and form your own support group. You could enlist your extended family to play a more supportive role in your child's life. Or you might check out the many community and church resources that are tailored to assist single parents and their kids.

Whatever you do, try to avoid the mind-set, "It's just you and me against the world, kid." Resist the tendency to let your child become your emotional support system—a prospect that can be scary for your child and unhealthy for both of you. Find some adult friends to help you keep your balance. Allow people into your life who can give you the support you need. And no matter what, remember that you're not alone, and you're not parenting alone. God is always with you, and he cares for you and your family.

6. Find the true basis of your self-worth.

Parents of spirited children can easily find themselves measuring their personal worth and significance by how well (or how poorly) their children are doing. But this is a one-way street to discouragement! Stop for a moment and ask yourself:

- What is the basis of my significance as a person?
- What is the basis for my security in life?

If your children are part of your answer, you're headed for trouble and lots of disappointment. As our own children grew older, we made a conscious decision not to base our sense of self-worth on how they turned out. Don't misunderstand us. We love our sons, and over the years family relationships have been very important to us. But we realized that basing our security and self-worth on decisions that our sons—and eventually their families—might make or not make was just setting ourselves up for heartache. Anytime we assume responsibility for things we can't control, we become candidates for anxiety.

What is the true basis of our significance as individuals? Our significance comes from our relationship with God and the fact that he created us in his own image. His love and acceptance of us is not based on how well we perform. How can anyone resist feeling significant if they really understand John 3:16: "For God so loved the world that he gave his one and only Son, that whoever believes in him shall not perish but have eternal life"?

What is the basis for our security? It's God's promise to never leave us or forsake us (Heb. 13:5). It doesn't matter if we win or lose, succeed or fail. God is totally faithful, and he's totally committed to us. If we understand that, could we be any more secure?

As parents, we need to make sure we're basing our personal security and sense of significance on our relationship with the Lord, not on how our spirited children perform. When our security and self-worth are set in God, we're free from the pressure of having to have perfect kids. We can love our children as they are and accept—even appreciate—their uniqueness. We can be patient and listen for their true feelings. We can resist the temptation to manipulate them. And we can entrust them with confidence to our loving heavenly Father.

7. Remember that it's the relationship that counts.

When the poet Robert Browning wrote, "The best is yet to be," he could have been talking about our family! As the years go by and we think back to our own active parenting days, we seem to remember

Age-*level* Characteristics

"Why won't my preschooler sit still and be quiet?" "Why is my elementary child so sensitive to criticism?" "Why is my teenager so moody?"

It's simply a stage they're going through!

Getting to know your children involves not only understanding childhood development stages, but helping them through those stages. What "unpleasant" behaviors, attitudes, and moods are normal, but temporary? What level of maturity can you expect of children at each stage of life? Use the following charts for insights into how to support and encourage your children's physical, mental, emotional, social, and spiritual growth.

Don't expect children to act like adults. Love them, accept them, and give them room to grow!

Preschool Characteristics

Physical

- Small, but growing
- Active—needs opportunity for movement
- Finger coordination isn't as developed as arm and leg coordination
- Boisterous and noisy
- Restless
- Loves repetition
- Susceptible to disease
- Sensitive eyes, ears, and voice
- Still needs lots of sleep

Mental

- Can learn a great deal, but has limits to understanding
- Doesn't differentiate between fantasy and reality
- Learns through senses
- Learns by asking questions (usually "why" or "how")
- Learns by imitation
- Displays increased verbal ability
- Has wide scope of interests
- Engages in much imaginary play
- Curious
- Doesn't think symbolically, but in concrete terms

Emotional

- Has ups—joy, warmth, sympathy, love
- Has downs—fear, anger, anxiety
- Insecure
- Is a show-off
- Developing sense of humor
- Physically aggressive, sometimes rough and careless with toys

Social

- Egocentric
- Struggles with authority
- Home-centered
- Beginning to be interested in friends
- Still has imaginary playmates

Spiritual

- Ideas about God are extensions of ideas about people (usually parents and teachers)
- Enjoys attending Sunday school
- Learning to pray
- Enjoys stories about Jesus
- Interested in God
- Gets Jesus and God confused

Primary Characteristics (Grades 1–2)

Physical

- Restless
- Loves strenuous activity
- Works hard; often overdoes
- Tires easily
- Is attempting to master a variety of new motor skills
- Willing to try anything without regard for danger
- Often stumbles and falls; awkward in movements
- Small muscle and eye-hand coordination developing; still clumsy in use of hands
- Seems to look everywhere at once; easily distracted
- Eyes easily strained from overuse
- Touches, handles, explores all materials within reach
- Expresses self through movement

Mental

- Attention span increasing, up to 20 minutes, but varying according to interest
- Differentiates between fantasy and reality
- Thinks in concrete terms
- Just beginning to develop reasoning ability
- Sphere of interest is widening
- Eager to learn
- Becomes excited about new learning tasks but may get discouraged in the middle and quit
- Can shift from one activity to another
- Recognizes sequence
- Has good memory when facts are presented in a meaningful context
- Likes to listen to stories
- Learns best by active participation, self-activation, and dramatic assimilation

Emotional

- Shifts between emotional extremes
- Needs routine, familiar surroundings
- Many new feelings are emerging
- Easily becomes angry at self, situations, others; younger primary may cry, have tantrum, become violent; older primary may sulk
- May set too high goals
- Ashamed of mistakes; irritated by failure
- May be defiant and rude, asserting independence from adult domination
- Responds negatively to direct demands, but benefits from reminders and verbal guidance
- Often inconsistent, indecisive when making difficult choice; when choice made, may be uncompromising

Social

- Shows loyalty, pride, and interests in family
- Attitudes vary toward brothers and sisters; may be bossy, jealous, proud, protective, or brutal
- Desires friends but does not get along well
- Has two or three best friends
- Wants to win
- Tries to dominate in social situations by showing off, acting silly, bullying others
- Critical of other children's behavior; tattles
- Desires attention; thrives on praise and approval
- Dislikes criticism
- Still quite self-centered

Spiritual

- Can grasp concept of God as Creator
- May ask questions—Who made God? Where is He?
- May fear God because God sees everything he does
- Developing a concept of God as a real person
- Sees Jesus as a real person
- Elementary awareness of who Jesus is
- Can grasp simple explanation that Jesus is the savior who died, came alive again, and someday will return to earth
- Understanding that Jesus took the blame for our wrongdoings
- Elementary understanding of sin; realizes he can choose right or wrong
- Recognizes Bible characters as real
- Considers prayer important

173

Middler Characteristics (Grades 3–4)
Physical

- High activity level; interested in games and organized activities such as baseball
- Fondness for rough, boisterous games
- Expresses himself in variety of postures, gestures, and stunts; more self-conscious in expression than earlier
- Increasingly fluid and graceful in bodily movements
- Courage and daring in physical activity; frequent accidents
- Less easily fatigued than earlier
- Increased speed and smoothness in fine motor performance; improved manipulatory ability; works very quickly and with increasing control

- Becoming better observer
- Interested in skill building; persistent in practicing complex motor skills
- Frequent repetition of enjoyed activities
- Drawing shows increasing awareness of body proportions; starting to draw in perspective; likes to draw figures in action
- Girls ahead of boys in physical development
- Able to take responsibility for personal hygiene

Mental

- Capable of prolonged interest and concentration
- Expresses amazement and curiosity
- Beginning to see patterns, contexts, and implications; universe becoming less disconnected
- Sees similarities because two things share observable features or abstract attributes
- Likes to plan ahead
- Good at memorizing short sentences; remembers better if something is written
- Enjoys reading
- Likes stories of fantasy, adventure, travel, faraway places, humor; comic books are favorites

- Increasing independence
- Does not like to fail, but likes to be challenged; does not become upset when tasks are difficult; persistent in completing tasks
- Older pupils make up mind rapidly, definitely
- Starting to apply logical thought to practical situations; mostly unsystematic, trial-and-error approach
- Understands concept of money

Emotional

- Shows definite signs of empathy
- Widely variable emotional behavior—shyness to boldness, morbid to cheerful, lethargic to excitable
- Likely to overextend self in thought and activities; when these become too much, he or she retreats, leaving "a mess"
- Often delays responses
- Anticipates with great eagerness; interest often short-lived; shifts rapidly
- Ready to tackle anything; likes challenges
- Feelings easily hurt; not given to prolonged depression; seeks reconciliation after being hurt

- Sensitive to criticism from adults
- Likes orderliness and neatness
- Frequently complains, sulks, mutters, "lets off steam" as outlet for tension
- May fear dark, fighting, and physical injury, failing, not being liked; often will not admit fears, even to self
- Worries frequently, often in midst of pleasant experiences
- Seeks friendly relationships with adults

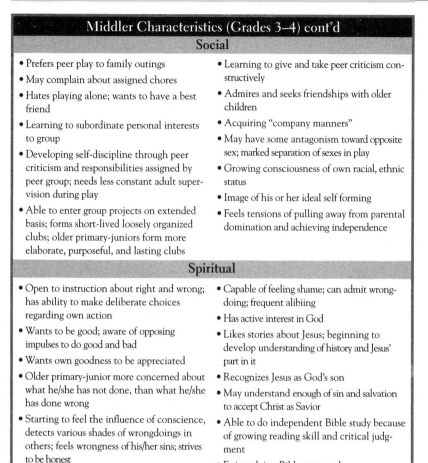

Middler Characteristics (Grades 3–4) cont'd
Social

- Prefers peer play to family outings
- May complain about assigned chores
- Hates playing alone; wants to have a best friend
- Learning to subordinate personal interests to group
- Developing self-discipline through peer criticism and responsibilities assigned by peer group; needs less constant adult supervision during play
- Able to enter group projects on extended basis; forms short-lived loosely organized clubs; older primary-juniors form more elaborate, purposeful, and lasting clubs

- Learning to give and take peer criticism constructively
- Admires and seeks friendships with older children
- Acquiring "company manners"
- May have some antagonism toward opposite sex; marked separation of sexes in play
- Growing consciousness of own racial, ethnic status
- Image of his or her ideal self forming
- Feels tensions of pulling away from parental domination and achieving independence

Spiritual

- Open to instruction about right and wrong; has ability to make deliberate choices regarding own action
- Wants to be good; aware of opposing impulses to do good and bad
- Wants own goodness to be appreciated
- Older primary-junior more concerned about what he/she has not done, than what he/she has done wrong
- Starting to feel the influence of conscience, detects various shades of wrongdoings in others; feels wrongness of his/her sins; strives to be honest

- Capable of feeling shame; can admit wrongdoing; frequent alibiing
- Has active interest in God
- Likes stories about Jesus; beginning to develop understanding of history and Jesus' part in it
- Recognizes Jesus as God's son
- May understand enough of sin and salvation to accept Christ as Savior
- Able to do independent Bible study because of growing reading skill and critical judgment
- Enjoys doing Bible map work

Junior Characteristics (Grades 5–6)

Physical

- High energy level
- Greater self-control and calmness in performing motor activities
- Improved ability to budget time; athletic ability greatly influences status with peers and self-concept
- Early physical maturing in boys and girls is related to more positive self-concept
- Girls begin preadolescent growth spurt; they are taller, heavier, often stronger than boys; often surpass boys in athletic prowess
- Girls starting to develop secondary sexual characteristics
- Quiescent growth period for boys

Mental

- Alert, eager to learn; younger junior may have short attention span
- Starting transition from concrete to abstract thinking
- Likes to identify facts and put items in order
- Likes to memorize
- Likes to read; enjoys stories
- Avid interest in history, people, current events, science, nature, geography
- Beginning to do independent, critical thinking; can consider why Bible characters acted as they did and why God dealt with them as He did
- Can apply logic to solving problems; starting to form hypotheses and test things

Emotional

- Younger junior generally cheerful, content, carefree, relaxed
- Older junior experiences more emotional peaks, more variable moods
- Younger junior oriented toward action rather than reflection; unselfconscious about feelings
- Older junior aware of feelings but does not understand their causes
- Strong feelings related to likes and dislikes
- Older junior sensitive to hurt feelings and criticism; subject to jealousy
- Occasional short-lived bursts of anger and violence
- Relieves tension through bodily movement
- Frequently bursts into laughter, especially when unsure of self

Social

- Wants many friends, but wants one best friend of same sex
- Girls prefer smaller more intimate peer groups; boys want larger, less close-knit groups
- Shares "secrets" and much personal information with friends
- Frequently fights and argues with peers
- Enjoys participating in gangs and clubs; spontaneous clubs are fluid in organization
- Enthusiastically participates in teams and games
- Respects teachers, taking their word over parents
- Thrives on certain amount of routine
- Exhibits best behavior away from home
- Loves teasing, chasing, pushing, hitting, nudging, poking, etc.

Spiritual

- Responsive to teaching about God's character
- Starting to realize he must follow his own convictions regarding Jesus
- Capable of understanding God's plan of salvation and Jesus' part in it; able to confess belief in Jesus and accept Him as Savior
- Understands the purpose of prayer; may make up spontaneous prayers
- Draws heroes from the Bible
- Primarily concerned with Bible facts
- Values belong to group; anxious to join church and be part of group
- Elementary understanding of ethical concepts
- Has strict moral code
- Capable of making value judgments about his/her own actions
- Often puzzled about right and wrong

176

Junior High Characteristics (Grades 7–9)

Physical

- Puberty—rapid growth and development
- Girls up to 2 1/2 years ahead of boys in growth
- Secondary sexual characteristics
- Girls: slow down in accumulation of fat—also experience skin changes; Boys: motor development, coordination improves
- Boys' self-image tied to physical development
- Boys' and girls' interests divergent

Mental

- Decrease in learning skills—28% get lower grades
- Concrete thinker—some abstract thinking
- Beginning to be an independent, critical thinker
- Questioning
- Increased use of logic, ability to think inductively
- Most understand things and concepts perceived by senses; less understanding of deep spiritual, metaphysical issues

Emotional

- Lack of self-confidence
- Overreacts, especially with parents; actually more in control of emotions than juniors
- Moody and unpredictable
- Often handles stress poorly
- Needs time alone, especially from parents
- Comes to grips with his/her male/female roles
- Often boisterous

Social

- Becoming independent of parents
- Conforms to group
- Strong peer attachments, especially to those of same sex
- Primary influence is peers; mother/father second; and then teachers

Spiritual

- Grappling with hard questions of his faith in order to "own" it
- Beginning to think beyond "self" to what it means to love others; beginning to develop a world view
- Needs to make significant contributions to church as part of ownership beginning to think of talents as service potential
- Patterns life responses to God after adult and peer models

177

Senior High Characteristics (9–12)

Physical

- Growth spurt for boys, resulting in awkwardness, reduction in self-esteem
- Special problems for boys with late growth spurts
- Secondary sex characteristics continue to develop
- Full physical development for both sexes—ages 17-19
- Overattention to physical appearance

Mental

- Great brain growth—some who pushed too hard in junior high will be unable to take advantage of their increased capabilities
- Interest in inductive, philosophical thinking
- Enjoys play with the hypothetical futurism
- Uses abstract rules to solve problems; thinks independently, critically, logically
- Asks difficult, faith-strengthening questions
- Language skills: Ability to clarify complex concepts; opinionated
- Considers career choices

Emotional

- Daydreaming common
- Emotional energy goes toward physical change; heterosexual relationships
- Worries about future, looks, grades, physical development
- Self is on center stage
- Increasing control of emotions
- Developing sensitivity to emotions of others
- Developing interest in poetry

Social

- Still achieving independence from parents
- Social group of primary importance
- Conflict between peer and adult roles
- Primary relationships between those of same sex
- Jobs and money play key roles in group acceptance, use of free time
- Developing socially acceptable behavior
- Some redeveloping relationships with parents

Spiritual

- Grappling with hard questions of faith in order to own it
- Beginning to show concern for others; very conscious of right and wrong in world situations
- Aware of self as model for junior highs
- Need to be accepted as contributing person of worth in own church; will accept significant projects, sometimes reaching beyond ability
- Concern for others can make him/her an effective witness

APPENDIX #2

What *kind of parent*
Are You?

An important key to really knowing and understanding our children is knowing *ourselves*. We need to understand how our unique personalities and parenting styles affect the way we relate to our children. Take a look at the information below and decide: Are you a reactive or adaptive parent? Public or private?

The Reactive Parent

Ask yourself the following questions:

- Do you tend to dominate your child and make all the decisions?
- Do you say things like, "Do this because I said so!" or "Don't question my authority. I'm the parent!"
- Do you often overreact to your child?
- Do you "major" on almost every issue, large and small?
- Do you struggle with being flexible?
- Are you directive; that is, do you make sure your kids know the rules and know where you stand on issues?

179

If you answered yes to most of these questions, you tend to be a reactive parent. You may need to work on relaxing, not taking life so seriously, and having some fun along the way. Stop occasionally, get down on the floor, and play with your toddler. Go for a walk with your child and enjoy the wildflowers!

And keep examining your priorities. Is a clean floor really more important than the excitement of the little boy who forgets to wipe his feet when he comes running in to show you the firefly he caught? Is a roll of toilet paper really more valuable than the creativity of the six-year-old sister who just set her brother's "broken arm" using toilet paper for gauze?

The Adaptive Parent

If you answered "no" to most of the previous questions, consider these:

- Do you go along with almost everything your child wants you to do?
- Do you have a hard time being assertive?
- Is it difficult for you to take charge?
- Do you like being "one of the kids"?
- Do you find that you don't major on the minors, but you don't major on the majors either?
- Is it easy to adjust to new situations?
- Do you fix different menus for your kids based on their likes and dislikes?

Did we just describe you? You tend to be an adaptive parent—one who is very loving and accepting but has difficulty asserting authority.

Allowing kids to make choices and have input into their own lives is good, but only to a point. A two-year-old doesn't have the expertise to run his or her life (not to mention everyone else's). A thirteen-year-old may think having a set bedtime is "for little kids," but he or she probably has no clue how much sleep a young teenager really needs. You need to work on recognizing situations in which parental control is necessary and learn to take charge.

As an adaptive parent who would rather be "just one of the kids," you probably have a lot of fun with your children. Even the teenage years are more enjoyable for you than they are for a more reactive parent. But be careful: It's easy for you to lose parental control before the appropriate time.

When our boys were growing up, I (Claudia) tended to be the reactive parent, while Dave tended to be the adaptive parent. I tended to see everything as a major issue, while Dave would ask, "What's the big deal?"

Spirited children see these style differences very clearly and will often play one parent against the other. That's why it's so important for moms and dads to recognize their individual tendencies and seek to work as a team. Together, Dave and I were able to find a healthy balance between being overly adaptive and overly rigid with our three sons. Our differences actually helped strengthen our parenting skills.

The Public Parent

If your house seems to have a revolving door, with neighborhood kids and your child's school friends going in and out at all times of the day or night, you just may be a public parent. You can be so much fun! You have a great time with your children and your children's friends. You tend to be activity oriented. You love people in general and children specifically.

You need to be careful, however, not to become so busy with other people and activities that you inadvertently neglect your own children. One young adult told us with a hint of sadness, "Everyone loved my mother, but she wasn't home a lot." You also need to resist the desire to push your more private children into activities just because you enjoy being so busy and involved.

The Private Parent

If you are creative, consistent, organized, and love to be alone, you are probably a private parent. When you're by yourself, you know you're in good company! You can get a lot accomplished, and you are seldom out of control. You need to be careful, however, not to become too detached, inflexible, or judgmental. You also need to avoid projecting your own perfectionist tendencies onto your children.

In our home we, as parents, were more public than private. At times, though, we loved the privacy of just being family or just being the two of us, without others involved. Our children were a combination—one was very public, one was very private, and one was in-between. Realizing how different each son was (both from us and from one another) helped us to avoid trying to push them into a single mold.

APPENDIX #3

Surviving *parent-teacher* Conferences

Do you feel nervous and apprehensive before a scheduled meeting with your spirited child's teacher? You're not alone. Parent-teacher conferences aren't known for being loads of fun! Why would you want to go into a situation in which the other person is likely to say something less than flattering about your son or daughter? You already know how difficult he or she can be—and you're the one who loves the child unconditionally! Besides, there's something inherently intimidating about going into a classroom—any classroom. Suddenly you're flooded with memories of your own school days, when you were the child and the teacher was the adult. It's hard not to feel like a child again when you're sitting on the other side of a teacher's desk!

Meet the Teacher

Hopefully the conference is not the first time you are meeting your child's teacher. When our boys were in school, we always tried to take advantage of open houses and parent-teacher association meetings to meet our boys' teachers at least briefly. We wanted our presence to show the teachers that we were interested in our children's schoolwork and that education was important in our family.

One parent told us, "We try to open a dialogue with our spirited child's teacher early on. We approach the school year as a team effort and the teacher as a key team member. We ask, 'How can we work together to make sure our child has a positive experience?' That team approach always goes a long way in getting the teacher on board to help us help our child."

Sharing Information

When you meet with your child's teacher, you may want to start with a few general questions, such as:

- Where is my child's desk?
- What is the grading scale?
- Will you give standardized tests? When are they given?
- What is the homework policy?
- How does my child relate to others in the class?

You also may want to share specific information that you think would be helpful for the teacher to know, such as:

- special situations at home;
- medical problems;
- your child's personal achievements beyond academics;
- how your child is motivated (for instance, by praise rather than reprimand).

Helpful Tips

Your parent-teacher conference may not be fun, but it can still be productive if you follow these five guidelines:

1. Make a list of topics you want to ask or talk about, and arrange your list so that the most important items are at

the top. Take the list with you and refer to it during the conference.

2. Be on time.

3. Keep a positive attitude. Remember that the goal of the meeting is to help your child.

4. Jot down the teacher's suggestions. Don't be afraid to ask questions about them.

5. Listen carefully to what the teacher says. Avoid any misunderstanding by paraphrasing back to the teacher what he or she has just said to you.

# Notes

Cry #1: "Look *at* Me!"

1. Adapted from the PEP Groups for Parents curriculum. David and Claudia Arp, *Building Positive Relationships for the Teen Years* (Colorado Springs: David C. Cook, 1994), 20.
2. Adapted from *Parent Talk* by Dr. Kevin Leman and Randy Carlson (Nashville: Thomas Nelson Publishers, 1993), 227–8.

Cry #2: "Did I *do* Good?"

1. *Building Family Strengths: A Manual for Families*, University of Nebraska—Lincoln, Department of Human Development and Family and Department of Conferences and Institutes, March 1986, 42.
2. Adapted from *Encouraging the Heart: A Leader's Guide to Rewarding and Recognizing Others* by James M. Kouzes and Barry Z. Posner (San Francisco: Jossey-Bass, 1999), 60.
3. Adele Faber and Elaine Mazlish, *How to Talk So Kids Will Listen and Listen So Kids Will Talk* (New York: Avon Books, 1982), 176.

Cry #3: "You're *not* Listening!"

1. Faber and Mazlish, *How to Talk*.

2. John Gottman, *Raising an Emotionally Intelligent Child* (New York: Simon and Schuster, 1997).

3. Donald Sloat, *The Dangers of Growing Up in a Christian Home* (Nashville: Thomas Nelson, 1986).

Cry #4: "I Want *to do it* My Way!"

1. Patricia Chamberlain and Gerald R. Patterson, "Discipline and Child Compliance in Parenting," included in *Handbook of Parenting*, M. H. Bornstein, ed. (Hillsdale, N.J.: Lawrence Erlbaum Associates, 1995), 4: 205–25.

2. Ross Greene, *The Explosive Child: A New Approach for Understanding and Parenting Easily Frustrated and "Chronically Inflexible" Children* (New York: HarperCollins, 1998).

3. T. Berry Brazelton, *Touchpoints: The Essential Reference* (Reading, Mass.: Perseus Books, 1992), 274–75.

4. Ibid.

5. Cynthia Ulrich Tobias, *You Can't Make Me—But I Can Be Persuaded* (Colorado Springs: WaterBook Press, 1999), 27.

6. Peter Goldenthal, "The Parent's Guide to Back-to-School Cool," *Woman's Day*, September 4, 1990, 120.

7. Claudia Arp, *Beating the Winter Blues: A Complete Survival Handbook for Moms* (Nashville: Thomas Nelson, 1991), 89.

Cry #5: "You *can't* Make Me!"

1. Lawrence Kutner, *Parent and Child* (New York: Morrow, 1991), 98.

2. Ibid, 145.

3. Brazelton, *Touchpoints*, 252.

4. Charlie Shedd, *Letters to Philip* (New York: Berkley Publishing, 1970).

5. Kevin Leman and Randy Carlson, *Parent Talk: Straight Answers to the Questions That Rattle Moms and Dads* (Nashville: Thomas Nelson, 1993), 17.

6. Kutner, *Parent and Child*, 146–7.

7. Shedd, *Letters to Philip*.

Cry #6: "I *hate* You!"

1. Adapted from *How to Really Love Your Children* by Ross Campbell (Wheaton, Ill.: Victor Books, 1981), 66–69.

2. Jean Illsley Clarke, *Self-Esteem: A Family Affair* (Center City, Md.: Hazelden Information and Educational Services, 1998).

Cry #7: "I *don't* Want To!"

1. Jerry White and Mary White, *When Your Kids Aren't Kids Anymore* (Colorado Springs: NavPress, 1989), 19.

2. Jean Lush with Pamela Vredevett, *Mothers and Sons* (Old Tappan, N.J.: Fleming H. Revell, 1988).

3. Linda Sonna, *The Homework Solution: Getting Kids to Do Their Homework* (Charlotte, Vt.: Williamson Publishing, 1990).

4. Kathy Collard Miller, "The Big R: Responsibility," *Christian Parenting Today*, May/June 1990, 40.

Cry #8: "I'm *a big kid* Already!"

1. Norm Wright, as quoted in *What Teenagers Wish Their Parents Knew about Kids* by Fritz Ridenour (Wheaton, Ill.: Victor Books, 1984), 157.

2. David and Claudia Arp, *Suddenly They're Thirteen* (Grand Rapids: Zondervan Publishers, 1999).

Other Resources *by* the Authors

Books

10 Great Dates to Energize Your Marriage

10 Great Dates Before You Say "I Do"

Love Life for Parents

The Second Half of Marriage

Empty Nesting

Suddenly They're 13

Quiet Whispers from God's Heart for Couples

52 Dates for You and Your Mate

Marriage Moments

Family Moments

The Big Book of Family Fun

Video Curricula

10 Great Dates to Energize Your Marriage

The Second Half of Marriage

PEP Groups for Moms

PEP Groups for Parents of Teens